THE JOURNEY

The Journey

The Story of Rose Warmer: courage,
faith and drama to rank with
The Hiding Place

by
MYRNA GRANT

HODDER AND STOUGHTON
LONDON   SYDNEY   AUCKLAND   TORONTO

British Library Cataloguing in Publication Data

Grant, Myrna
  The journey.
  1. Warmer, Rose 2. Converts from Judaism
  – Biography 3. World War, 1939-1945 – Jews
  I. Title
  940.53'1503'924   BV2623.W/

  ISBN 0 340 24007 5

CONTENTS

Eden Lost

I WAS FIVE YEARS OLD in 1914 when I heard the word "war." At first it seemed to me that something wonderful had happened. In spite of the July heat, people were running all over the resort lawns, leaping up from their chairs under the trees, forming small excited clusters, and then scattering in all directions. The tennis courts were emptied. Robed, barefooted guests using the spas bounded out of the clinics and joined the throng of summer dresses and white trousers swirling in jubilation.

From somewhere a man appeared waving a newspaper. He jumped onto the veranda of a villa, holding the paper above his head with both hands, screaming the headlines in a delirium of joy: "Austria-Hungary declares war on Serbia!"

Everyone began cheering and embracing. I ran to my mother in delight. She was standing quietly with some other members of Pieštany's staff, holding my little brother's hand. I could see her searching the crowds, and I knew she was looking for my father who had gone into town for electrical supplies. Finally we saw father rushing toward us, his workers and apprentices pushing around him. Beads of perspiration fringed his thick eyebrows and brief moustache.

"The city is in an uproar," he was saying breathlessly. "There is cheering and dancing in the streets, flags everywhere." He greeted mother with his eyes and pulled out his huge white handkerchief to wipe his forehead as he talked. "People say Belgrade will be captured within a week, that it is a new day for the Austro-Hungarian empire!"

A portly guest in an elegant jacket who had joined our group began to cheer. He was a man I had once thought to be the Emperor Franz Joseph himself, because he had come to Piešťany in a magnificent carriage. My mother had laughed at me, but the fact was we frequently had nobility as guests. The splendor of the grounds, the health-giving mineral spas, the clinic with its staff of agreeable doctors and therapists drew many of the world's richest and most famous people.

The staff and the guests were always on easy terms, but today there seemed no distinction at all. Everyone and everything seemed delightfully mixed together.

Earlier that same summer there had been another day of commotion at Piešťany, as different from this one as it was possible to be. The Archduke Ferdinand of Austria had been shot, and I saw my mother press her hand to her chest as if she had been hurt. Piešťany had been silent on that June day. The guests who had come early in the season stayed in the hotel or the smaller villas, and I heard weeping and whispering, and there was anger in the air.

Now, all was celebration. On someone's order, waiters began carrying out silver trays of fragile champagne glasses to the tables under the trees. There was a wonderful popping of corks. People began singing.

> *Up, Hungarians! It's your country calling!*
> *Now's the moment, now or never!*
> *Shall we be slaves? Shall we be free?*
> *That's the question—what's your answer?*
> *In God's great Name we swear, we swear,*
> *No more shall we be slaves—no more!*

Everyone was swept up in a passion of patriotism. How long it all went on I can't imagine, but finally, spent with enthusiasm, the doctors, chambermaids, kitchen helpers, therapists, housekeepers drifted back to their posts of duty, exalted beyond measure and making plans.

Father disappeared with his apprentices. Mother turned toward our flat in the city, taking me firmly by one hand and my little brother, Joseph, by the other. The resort area where my father was chief electrician was actually both an island in a river and a great mainland park, the two parts joined by a high and ancient bridge. To get home, we had to walk from the island, over the bridge and all the way through the park. It was a walk I loved and mother often let me dawdle, watching patiently while I chased butterflies or gazed down at swimmers in the swift river under the bridge.

Today there were no swimmers, and mother wouldn't let us play. Our progress was so purposeful, I asked if we were going to the synagogue. Poppa had long ago left off going to synagogue, but in those early years Momma still went. Frequently she took several of us children with her, and there was no playing in the park on the way.

I had an idea that Momma's attendance at synagogue had something to do with her large family living in nearby Budapest. They seemed to make a great deal more out of being Jewish than we did.

How my grandmother, Julia, would fuss when she came to Piešťany with grandfather to visit. "I can't eat in a house that isn't kosher!" she would declare, shooing my mother out of the kitchen. I think she brought her own dishes in a big basket. There would be a great clatter of china and pans, and then for as long as they stayed grandmother would do the cooking and the washing up.

When our grandparents visited, all of us children loved the suddenly imposed ritual of standing around the dinner table while grandfather recited the blessing on the bread. And we would pray again, a longer prayer, when the meal was over.

By this time, our family was complete—four boys and two girls. Joseph, next to me in age, was the baby of the family and my constant playmate. My sister, Felice, at eleven, was a mother's dream. During Grandmother Julia's occupation of the kitchen, Felice spent many hours helping. "The stomach carries the feet," grandmother was fond of saying with a wise smile at

Felice. The three older boys seemed remote to me and absorbed in an almost grown-up world of study.

"Of course we are not going to synagogue today!" Mother's answer was cut short by a burst of cheering as she hurried Joseph and me along. We were passing through the center of the park where there were many little cafes, each with a small, easeful orchestra of its own.

Ordinarily people would sit outside for hours at the small cafe tables under striped umbrellas, sipping coffee and eating pastries, and talking. The musicians would play from late morning until late night.

On this day, the music was brisk and loud, and I looked down the road to see if a parade was coming. Men crowded the cafes, standing and shouting. No one noticed us passing by, and Momma didn't look to see if there were friends to wave to.

Dinner that night was disappointing after the excitement of the day. Poppa was careful as usual to give the first slice of meat to the girl who lived with us and helped mother. "It's part of her wages," he would explain if a guest raised an eyebrow. Father also insisted that our maid be treated with absolute courtesy at all times. He was an exacting man, a perfectionist in his work as chief electrician at Pieštany and with his family as well. We all tried hard to please him. Yet when he went off to the city on business, as he had done today, he almost always brought back a small treat of some kind for us children.

Most of father's relatives lived in Vienna and Momma's in Budapest. The subdued talk that night around the table no doubt involved concern for how the war might affect the lives of everyone in our large Jewish family, scattered over Austria and Hungary. Father had six sisters. He was the only son, orphaned when young and brought up by his grandparents. His grandfather, Felix, had been a teacher and journalist in Vienna, who because of his profession mixed freely with Gentiles. He did not keep the Jewish traditions; so my father, who left grandfather's home early, went to Germany to learn how to be an electrician, making friends outside the Jewish communities. In spite of his lack of religion, in all his life I never heard my father speak against God, even with all that was to come upon us. I heard him say plenty, though, against Jewish men who went to synagogue and while there, in between their prayers, chatted about trivial things or even conducted business!

My mother and her brothers and sister, Caroline, had been raised in a very old Hungarian town that was a Roman Catholic bishopric. Her brothers all went to university in that town; and because it was an academic center, my mother and her sister had opportunity to go all the way through high school, as far as girls could advance in those days.

Her mother, my Grandmother Julia, had always kept a kosher household and in spite of the fact that mother didn't, our family ties were very close. Relatives from both sides of our huge family were always visiting us at Piešťany. "Who is rich? He who enjoys his riches!" one of my uncles would say as he stretched out under the lush trees of Piešťany.

Would war change everything? Poppa didn't think so; it would be over quickly, and our family would be safe at the resort. Poppa assured mother he would not be drafted into the army. He was Piešťany's chief electrician, with many apprentices and total responsibility for the lighting of all the villas, hotels, and spas. Poppa said he would be surprised anyway if the war lasted more than a few weeks. How could Serbia and backward Russia and little France and England stand for long against the combined might of Germany, Austro-Hungary, and the whole Ottoman Empire?

Momma had a face like a valentine and wore her rich dark hair waved up and back from her broad forehead. I was glad that she seemed reassured by my father's answer. She passed him his coffee cup with a sigh of relief. Her high school sons would not grow up to go to war.

But the fighting didn't end in a few weeks, and as the months passed, things did change at Piešťany. Now there were new and cheap buildings at the resort, hastily erected for wounded soldiers who needed our hot springs and physiotherapists to recover. Officers occupied the hotels along with civilian guests. I thought it was wonderful to see their uniforms and plumed metal helmets that flashed with color as they walked. Even the regular soldiers' blue uniforms with red piping looked smart. Often they played games with us staff children. We chased as we liked through the hotels and cafes, playing war and pretending to capture the English.

11

With the turning of the leaves in the autumn, my brief life also changed: I started school. Because my father was strict, I was terrified of my teacher and silent in class. But after school I made friends easily and became the leader of a band of small children who loved the out-of-doors as much as I did. Gradually I lost some of my fear, and school became bearable and even interesting. Time that had hung so slowly over every painful hour of instruction soon passed more quickly. Eventually, longed-for and beloved summer came at last. I felt myself to be a bird, soaring out of the confines of the school into the freedom of the park and river and the deep woods beyond that. The war everyone talked about seemed very far away.

But to my parents it came home. It was the time of my oldest brother, Eugene's, graduation from high school in Budapest. To mother's horror, immediately he was taken to serve the Kaiser in the army. Every young boy in his class was conscripted and they all left the city together, singing songs, marching off, awkward and pleased in their scratchy uniforms.

Ordinary food became very expensive. My mother and Felice worked hard in our garden, coaxing every inch of earth to yield potatoes or onions or cabbages for our winter table. Our maid seemed forever on her feet in front of the kitchen stove in a haze of steam, stirring the huge pan that Momma used for making jam and preserving fruit. After only a year, most of Poppa's workers and apprentices had gone to war. Poppa's working hours became endless, and all the grown-ups seemed tired and determined and bewildered that the war was lasting so long.

But for us younger children it was summer! In the mornings, wearing only our bathing suits, we would race to the river to spend the whole day swimming in its icy mountain water. Often we'd take sandwiches and some fruit with us. When we were shaking with cold and could no longer warm ourselves in the slanting sun of the late afternoon, we would hurry back to Pieśťany to the hot spas and jump into the steaming mineral baths. The therapists loved us children and would bundle us into towels and rub our blue skins until they tingled. When we were warm again, we would often run back to the river for one last swim before dusk.

My younger brother, Joseph, and I had to play hard to keep up

12

with the older children. Perhaps it was because of the competition that I became a good athlete at a young age. Also, at Piešťany we were exposed to the constant emphasis on sports and fitness and bodybuilding. Even in the wintertime we had guests who would come for sports and exercise and therapy.

I remember one day of bitter cold the first winter of the war. My sister, Felice, and her friends were going skating, and I begged my mother to make her take me along. The river was solid with ice and because I couldn't yet skate, the older children took me out to the middle of the river, strapped on my skates, and in a flash of blades raced off. In moments they were no more than whirling patches of color against the white landscape, too far away to even hear my terrified entreaties.

After a while, I pulled my handkerchief out of my coat pocket and with mittened clumsiness unfolded it, laid it on the ice, and carefully sat down. Soon I was very cold and began to cry. Felice paid no attention. I could see she wasn't giving me a glance, even though I never took my pleading eyes from her as she circled gracefully with her friends. There was nothing to do but get up. Finally I found the courage to push my wobbly ankles across the ice. I discovered with astonishment that I was skating! I was entranced by the floating movement and the gliding freedom and the sudden admiration of Felice and the other children. As I tried other sports, I found I became quickly accomplished in all of them.

My body had to be constantly active. My mind, too, leapt from one thing to another. I was constantly asking questions, pestering all the people around me for answers. My father's language was German, so all of us children spoke it easily, as well as our native Hungarian. As soon as I learned to read, I devoured children's books in both languages but found them unsatisfying.

"Thou hast added water, add flour also," Poppa would quote an old saying when my questions finally provoked him. He meant that in addition to constantly asking, I ought to try to add something relevant to my conversation.

Like all children, I wondered about God. Our little town near the resort was divided into an old part and a new. In the old part was an impassive Roman Catholic church. On the top of its steeple shone a gold cross. Hundreds of feet below the cross in the church square was a stone pillar where, I was told, sinners were bound in olden times. Christians going to Mass on Sunday mornings would have had to walk past offenders lashed to the cold stone. I was shocked that human beings could have been treated in such a way.

In our park were niches with religious statues and crosses. Often I would see people kneeling before them (a sight which grieved my mother), sometimes weeping but always looking very sad. Over and over the people would make the sign of the cross. I was happy not to be under that fearful sign. At least our Jewish God helped us and gave us bread and seemed generally easy to please.

One religious incident in those early years touched me deeply. In our city was a Christian family I liked very much. Although the father was a millionaire, he was a humble man, and instead of renting a villa on the island, he stayed with his family in a modest summer house in the town. They walked to the island to take the waters and then returned home. They had five children, one a young daughter my own age, and we played together. One day the father gave me a little book called, *Give Us This Day Our Daily Bread*. The book affected me profoundly. In the quiet of the Scriptures I had never seen before, I was nourished for awhile.

But that book was soon neglected. Our home was full of other books, and all of us loved to read. Unfortunately, getting permission to read was another thing. My father firmly believed that children ought to learn obedience to duty. After school and on weekends we had tasks to do. It didn't matter that my mother always had women employed to help her with the work. We children worked too, and my parents' standards were exacting. Housekeeping was hard in those days. There were no canned foods or supermarkets or machines to do heavy work. As the war went on, the gathering and cooking and preserving of food became increasingly difficult.

Even the washing of clothes required a woman to come every day. Early in the morning she would roll up her sleeves in the wash shed behind our flat and light the fire under my mother's huge tub. I loved the steamy smell of wet wood and strong soap and the sounds of cracking logs and the thumping of the long pole as she stirred and pounded the boiling clothes and tablecloths and billowing, bubbling bed sheets. By noon our lines of laundry would be flapping madly in the river wind. In the winter months, we had to drag the baskets of water-heavy laundry to the attic of the building next door and hang the clothes there. Even indoors, the cloth often froze solid. I hated the way we had to smash the stiff shirts and dresses to fold them into our hampers. I imagined they were crying out.

When the day's work was finally done and lessons finished, then Poppa permitted me to read. No book on our crowded shelves was forbidden and very early I began to read Goethe, Schiller, Thomas Mann, Hesse.

As the war continued, I could sense despair deepening. The air seemed somehow thickened with it, and one breathed it in and felt dark and tired. In the pages of our books, men spoke to this despair. I struggled over Nietzsche's strange writings with consternation. "Thus far," he asserted, "no one has in the least doubted or hesitated to claim a higher value for the 'good' than for the 'evil.' What if the opposite were true? What if in the 'good' there were a symptom of regression, also a danger, a temptation, a poison, a narcotic. . . . Can it be possible that the supreme danger should be morality?" Nietzsche called upon man to be stronger, less bound by conventional morality, free from restrictions. What could it mean?

Perhaps my parents had not read these books or if they had, the sight of their young daughter puzzling over big words caused them no alarm. Surely such books would improve my vocabulary and my reading ability. But I know now that the ideas I was absorbing, however cloudily, page by page, were to poison me in later years. Even as a child, I felt compelled by them to defy convention and authority.

In our small Jewish school we had every day what we called "Religious Hour." We were taught the Hebrew alphabet and had to read a little from simple passages in the Old Testament. I loved Hebrew and felt superior because I learned it easily. One day we had to read the opening verses of the book of Genesis. "In the beginning God created the heavens and the earth." After class on that day I called all the children around me outside the school. "What we read in school is a lie," I declared. My friends stared at me in fearful disbelief. It was a dramatic moment and I made the most of it. "It is a lie because—there IS no God!" I was delighted at the sensation I caused.

It is the nature of childhood to be oblivious to inconsistency. At the same time that I was reading my parents' books and showing off to my classmates, I entered fully into Jewish religious life when I visited my Aunt Caroline in Budapest. Her husband was a prosperous shopkeeper and since they were childless, they frequently asked my parents to let one or another of us children stay with them for a time.

My aunt and uncle's home was strictly Orthodox, and there was much about the order and ritual of their household that inexplicably I liked. I especially loved the Sabbath, when I would be expected to appear for our Sabbath meal dressed in my best dress for the blessings over light and wine. My aunt's table was set with her finest linens. The china glowed in the golden Sabbath candles. There were the traditional twisted loaves, stuffed fish, and treats that did not appear even on my aunt's ample table on other days of the week. I sang the pleasantly syncopated Sabbath table hymns, and my Aunt Caroline would smile at my happy singing and take her ease.

Being childless, my aunt unfortunately knew nothing about living with children, but she had plenty of opinions on how children ought to behave. During the week she was impossible to please. If I sat one way, she would tell me to sit another. My foot wasn't in the right place, my dress had a wrinkle, my expression was wrong, my fork wasn't held at the correct angle. In my aunt's house, no bread could be eaten (except the Sabbath loaves) because Aunt Caroline said it made one stupid. Clearly I had eaten bread at home!

My uncle went to synagogue every evening, a practice I considered excessive. I think it was pleasant for my uncle who relaxed in the cafes after prayers, and spent long hours playing cards there with his friends.

There was a lot of praying in my Aunt Caroline's house. Before breakfast in the mornings, I had to recite prayers for half an hour. If I began late and had to leave for school as soon as they were completed, I went without breakfast. Even so, I didn't become angry. It seemed right to me that the prayers were more important than the food.

16

But as I grew older, I became rebellious. At home I believed the brilliant nihilism I read about in our books. I felt my father's practical atheism admirable. For one thing, I knew he was a better man than my uncle, in spite of my uncle's daily attendance at synagogue. And at Piešťany no one was interested in God except Momma. Sometimes she took her prayer book to the end of the park by the river's edge where our forest began. Surrounded by the perfection of nature, she would pray. Even in the distance my eyes could catch the sun glinting off the silver and white of her prayer book cover.

I was inwardly torn, my mind nakedly exposed to Nietzsche and the other authors, my child's heart longing for a shelter. To conquer my heart, I more and more rejected any authority. If I was ordered to do anything, that would be the very thing I would refuse to do.

Once at my Aunt Caroline's I bought a copybook I needed for school with some birthday money I had been given. My aunt was angry at the purchase and assumed I had procured the book by some devious means. The insistence of her voice cut through me.

"Rose, you tell me where you got the money for that copybook!"

I opened my mouth to protest, then clamped it shut.

"You will be punished if you do not answer. Where did you get that money?"

I pressed my lips together, my face flaming in indignation.

My uncle, hearing the commotion, soon joined the interrogation with considerable irritation. Frustrated at my stubborn silence, he shouted at me. I held my breath. I was furious at the suspicion in their faces and their insistence that I explain.

The inevitable beating occurred. I tried at first not to cry out, but soon I was sobbing and shocked. Still I would not tell. I knew I was in the right and that my aunt and uncle were wrong, and I would not open my mouth to speak.

Finally, they became frightened and took me to an old relative nearby they knew I loved. She gave them tea and then led me into another room and sat with me on a couch. She put her arm around me and patted my hand. I poured out the story of the birthday money and showed her the change that was still in my pocket.

My mother would never have thought of beating a child, but

all the same when she tried to order me to do something, and I didn't want to do it, I found ways of pestering her so that I did not have to do it.

Someday I would learn everything there is to know about taking orders.

As 1916 dragged into 1917, our world reeled with disasters. There was revolution in Russia. Czar Nicholas abdicated. The United States entered the war on the side of France and England. Food disappeared. We all began to lose weight. "Meatless weeks" became "meatless months," and we knew that some were starving. Stores were empty and hospitals full. People seemed to know the unthinkable: we were losing and the war would soon be over.

It ended on November 11, 1918, but the Armistice signed on that day did not bring relief to our desperate country. Now revolution raged over Hungary too, and Franz Joseph's successor, Emperor Karl, was deposed. Our Habsburgs were gone as surely but not as tragically as the Romanoffs in Russia, and with the revolution came the collapse of our historic union with Austria. Hungary became an independent republic. The old Empire was no more. Hungary was alone and near collapse.

Throughout Europe there arose a destructive fever. All the old ways of life fell away with the end of the monarchies. Ancient demonic forces were unleashed. For all Jews it was a time of fear. A reason had to be found to explain the fall of the German alliance. How was it possible that the combined might of the German, Austro-Hungarian, and Ottoman Empires had been defeated by the puny West? There was an explanation: treason from within. And who if not the Jews were the traitors? Terrible lies were circulated: the Jews had been unwilling to fight; they had used the war for personal profit; they avoided fighting at the front; they were parasites, sucking the lifeblood of every country in which they lived.

Throughout Hungary we had desperate shortages of everything. Thousands of people couldn't find any sort of job, and thousands more were sick and dying from a virulent influenza that devoured all Europe. Everyone was hungry and cold. Mobs formed in the streets. It was the Jews who were to blame for all the suffering.

I was nine years old when I first heard these things. I listened to my uncles and my father discussing them, poring over the German language papers my father had once loved, protesting what was called "the Jewish question." My mother heard, her face showing absolute stillness.

Whisperings told of horrifying things. In the provinces pogroms were begun. Hundreds of Jews were massacred in village after village. In the cities, Jews were fired from government jobs. Universities put quotas on the number of Jewish students they would accept. Even in Piešťany people looked at our family with resentment. I began to cry at night.

In the bitter border disputes following the war, it happened that an area of Hungary had to be annexed to the Czechoslovakian Republic. It was the part of our country that included Piešťany. We were Hungarians. We had suffered for our beloved country. Our soldiers had died for Hungary. And now suddenly we were expected to be Czechoslovakians.

Everything fell apart. My school was closed. People began moving away in huge numbers, and waves of new people moved into our city. The familiar government officials were gone and new ones were in charge. But worst of all, we had to speak Czechoslovakian. Like true Hungarians, our family rebelled. The idea of giving up our own language was unthinkable, but eventually we were officially forced to do it. It was forbidden to speak Hungarian even on the street, and in our homes we were supposed to speak only Czech or Slovak so all would learn. Poor father had never even learned Hungarian well. He always spoke to us in German. Now he was expected to speak nothing but a completely new language.

When my school opened again, I had a very bad time. With my rebellious nature, I fought against anything Czech and was punished constantly. My teacher was always angry at me. I was wretchedly unhappy. It would have been easy for me to learn Czech. I already knew German and Hungarian and had learned Slovak from the guests at Piešťany. But I doggedly refused. Eventually, of course, I had to give in.

In those difficult years after the war, many changes came to our family, even though somehow we continued to live at Piešťany. My father had trained my brothers, Louis and Herman, as electricians. He had insisted on perfection from them, with the result that my brothers were very skilled at the end of their training. It was a shock to my mother when Louis, her third son, decided at age twenty-one to emigrate with his skills to America. He comforted her that he would be able to come home to visit, but Mother had a terrible premonition she would never see him again—and she was right.

My brother Herman got married soon after Louis left and also moved away. He opened an electrical shop and worked in a neighboring town before moving to Prague. But Louis in America persuaded Herman and his young wife to join him in his new land. And so my parents saw another son set sail from the shores of Europe.

For a time even my father wanted to emigrate, but my mother wouldn't consider it, even with two sons in the United States. All of her big family lived in Budapest or towns even closer to Piešťany, and she couldn't remove herself from them. By this time my oldest brother, Eugene, was studying to become a medical doctor, and we were all terribly proud of him. *He* wasn't emigrating to America and so with all these things on her mind, mother said no. If she and Poppa had gone, it would have saved their lives.

In our town there was no high school; so when I was fourteen, I finished the education that was available to me. It was a stormy time. I was restless and increasingly stubborn, full of unhappy longings I didn't understand and couldn't express. I remember roaming for hours through the forests beyond the resort, yearning for something far better than what I had. Even books lost interest for me and often when I tried to read, the book would drop out of my hands and I would find myself pretending that I was dressed up like a sheep boy and traveling all over the world. No one would know I was a girl, and I imagined trains and foreign ships and strange places.

There was a woman in our town who had been a French teacher for very rich people in Turkey. To occupy me, my parents arranged that she should come to our home and teach me French. At that time, the whole world spoke French, and I was eager to master it. I worked hours every day studying what she taught me. I suppose it made up a little for the loss I felt in not being able to go to high school.

I also began the study of music with piano lessons. We didn't have a piano in our home, but the villas and hotels had plenty of pianos, and I practiced on them when I pleased.

My doctor brother Eugene often came home to visit us (for a while he actually worked in Piešťany, but he didn't like it because nobody was really sick). During my teen years, he helped me with my French and tried to encourage me to be disciplined and to learn anything that was available to me. He arranged for me to take a commerical course in a little local school; I learned how to type and to do office work.

For the most part I spent my days helping my mother at home and entering more and more into the postwar social life of Piešťany. There were lots of parties and sports activities and outings for young people, and I didn't lack for amusement. There was even a free movie theater, so I saw a great many films. We all went whenever we liked. I cheered up and thought perhaps the future would be bright after all.

I began to be admired for my athletic daredevilry and for the books I had read and the languages I could speak, and for my endless energy and ingenuity in finding outrageous things to do. By the time I was eighteen I informed my mother that I was engaged, but soon broke it off, an escapade that deeply horrified her sense of propriety.

At this time Eugene decided it was time to take me in hand. I think he understood that my madcap activity was a way of expressing the bottled up dreams and ambitions and longings inside of me. He devised a plan for me to go to Vienna and study physical education. Often he had seen me doing acrobatics on the rails of the bridge at Piešťany. Hundreds of feet below, the river swirled over the rocks and I loved to make onlookers gasp in fear. If someone was drowning, it was nothing to me to dive into the river and pull him out. I didn't know that drowning people could pull rescuers under, and if I had known I wouldn't have cared.

Perhaps my parents thought I would be safer studying in Vienna than showing off in Piešťany. At any rate, it was decided that I would go, with Eugene paying for my studies. At that time physical education courses were entirely different than they are now. In my youth, such studies included dancing, ballet, and gymnastics as well. I would learn theory at the famous Art Academy in Vienna and would practice gymnastics and dance on its very stage. It sounded wonderful to me. And so, as a young girl, I plunged into the very center of Europe's festering intellectual and cultural life. I was in Vienna. It was 1927, and I was eighteen years old.

II

The Fall

I HAD COME to my father's city, a place I had heard of all my life. It was with the joy of recognition that I first saw the coffeehouses, the theaters, parks, governmental buildings, some still embossed with the K.K., signifying the *Kaiserlich Königlich*, the imperial royalty of Franz Joseph and the Austro-Hungarian Empire, even though all that was now part of history.

I quickly came to love the homey gentle properness that pervaded Viennese social life—the soft-spoken German, the *Auf wiedersehn* of "until we meet again," and the *Servus*, "at your service," in parting. People wished me *Alles gute*, "may all be good," or *Alles in butter*, a phrase which delighted me and means prosperity, having to do with the rich Viennese cooking, which seemed to begin and end in butter or cream.

It wasn't long before I had found my own favorite coffeehouse where I could meet with my new friends from the Art Academy. Students worked very hard in Vienna, but there was always time for sitting around in the coffeehouses over *Kleinen Braunen*, the fragrant small coffees with milk, to argue philosophy and art and politics, our enthusiasm irritating carefully dressed gentlemen reading their newspapers or playing cards.

And over all of life was a lovely looseness, a denial of *verboten*, "forbidden." The somber and unsettling war years of my childhood were over forever. Ahead for me glittered success and fame and great happiness.

I was not only in a new city, I was in a new world. I bought a lipstick and liked the way I looked. I went to every play or concert I could possibly afford, and when I didn't have money for a seat I would buy a "standing ticket" and spend the evening on my feet transported by the magnificence and tragedy of the music or drama that penetrated and shook and lifted my very soul.

At the Academy, dance was the major part of our training and every day meant painful hours exercising at the bar. But ballet was not so important in our course as the form of dance called expressionism, created in America and made popular in Europe by the great dancer Isadora Duncan. The same year I came to Vienna, she was tragically killed in Paris when her flowing scarf caught in the wheel of the open car in which she was riding. She had just completed a triumphant concert and was at the height of her career. Everyone at the Vienna Art Academy grieved for her. We students threw ourselves with even more passion into her dance form, a technique actually based on Greek art.

Often in the very early mornings of spring and summer, I would go to the Danube and dance barefooted along the banks. I loved the wetness of the grass under my feet and the swirling of my dress around my legs and body. Dance was like prayer to me. It was an expression of my whole being, a way of abandoning myself to the inner longing that seemed to have been unsatisfied in me all of my life.

One April evening in Vienna, I happened to go alone to an oratorio at the Concert Hall. I was very tired and sank into my seat more asleep than awake. Idly I glanced at the program the usher had thrust into my hand. "St. Matthew Passion by Bach." I closed my eyes thankfully. Bach would be worth coming for.

As the curtain rose in front of the two great choirs who were to sing and the first sweeping orchestral themes filled the Hall, I was instantly awake, shaken by the inner knowledge that something of vast importance was about to take place. The opening words pierced my soul like an arrow: "Come my daughter, share my mourning!" All the world's sorrows seemed to be contained in the music. I began to tremble. I knew I was that daughter and that the invitation was to me. With mounting grief I listened as the passion of Christ unfolded. I had never read the New Testament. Never before had I heard this epic tragedy, exalted now as it was by the soaring music, the ancient German hymns, the profound dignity of the text.

I left the Concert Hall that night shaken with a terrible sorrow I did not understand. With all my heart I wanted to *do* something, but there was nothing I knew to do.

Soon enough the experience faded and was put aside as indifferently as I had put aside the small book that had stirred me so deeply in my childhood.

At the Art Academy were students from every walk of life. Sons and daughters of nobility studied with young people whose fathers might be bakers or (as in my case) electricians. Many professional class families sent their children to the Academy for polish. We danced, exercised, studied, dreamed, loved, worried, quarreled like students everywhere. I became as popular a madcap in Vienna as I had been in Piešťany, and the atmosphere of "anything goes" suited me exactly. I found that I could kick off my shoes and dance anywhere, anytime, even without music; that I could express myself with my body so that people understood it and loved it.

There were often parties in wealthy homes, and always I was urged to dance. People would follow me through the rooms as I leaped and swirled and soared as easily as if the rooms were an empty stage and an orchestra were filling my soul with music.

One magic winter weekend in 1928, I was invited with a group of doctors to a conference at the Semering resort, a place of magnificent elegance. During the mornings there were a few lectures, but later there were winter activities—skating, sledding, races, skiing. It was the peak of winter sports. For those who preferred to stay indoors, card games and chess were played on tables placed in front of blazing fireplaces. In the evenings there were entertainments of small concerts or dancing. Meals were lavish affairs. Lake fish, veal, wild mushrooms, sausages of all kinds and sizes, fowl, soups rich with tiny dumplings, shredded cabbage cooked in sour cream were served. Cakes of every kind abounded, and plates of pastries were presented with urns of thick whipped cream.

One afternoon of that weekend it began snowing. Suddenly I felt the impulse to make something from snow. I pulled on my boots and gloves, snatched my coat from the cloakroom, and rushed outside. All afternoon I worked, sculpturing in the snow, oblivious to the cold wind that came up. What a sudden power I felt in my hands! What joy in molding the snow, pressing and coaxing and smoothing it into human features, arms, bodies, eyelids, Finally my fingers were too stiff to move and I had to come in. But the excitement of what I had done stayed with me and I immediately embarked on a new study in Vienna, that of sculpting.

I began to work hard and discovered that I could express my soul with my fingertips as well as with my dancing body. Wet clay under my hands became wing tips and claws, hooves, a lion's flank, a child's hand, a human face. It could become sadness and anger and longing and laughter. It became music.

My graduation from the Art Academy in the summer of 1929 came as a shock. It was almost as if a beautiful concert abruptly stopped in the middle. I was unfinished, torn away from the concert stage, the gymnasium, the cafes, and parties and concerts. No longer would I stroll down the lovely streets studying the wonderful outdoor sculptures as I went, or cross the Franz Joseph Platz to gaze at the royal palace and the Byzantine court church. I felt I had barely begun in Vienna, but all the same I had my diploma and no excuse in the world not to get on the train that would take me to the lush seclusion of Piešťany and my quiet family.

My sister Felice had stayed at Piešťany and was now on the staff, putting her wonderfully practical nature to good use in managing the sanatorium. Soon she was indispensable and much admired for her efficiency. She viewed my newly-won Viennese diploma with a skeptical eye.

"Your dancing is very beautiful, Rose," she would say, "but you've got to have something practical on hand. You can't make a living leaping around the riverbanks!"

Felice wanted me to begin a course in physiotherapy at the sanatorium. When she talked about it, I made terrible faces and ran off to swim. Then she suggested I go to Sweden and study massage. Even worse! Finally I agreed to work at the sanatorium helping the doctors and teaching gymnastics to the guests. I actually developed a flourishing little school that summer and earned a lot of money. I worked hard when I finally understood why Felice was so concerned that I be able to support myself.

Although my parents represented the poorer branch of our prosperous family, we had always lived comfortably, except in the last years of the war when even the richest people suffered. But while I had been studying in Vienna at my brother's expense, my father had invested his savings and some of my brother's money in the building of a new sanatorium in Piešťany. Before it could be finished, the owner declared bankruptcy and my father lost everything. He and my mother and Felice moved from the resort where they had lived since the war back to a flat in the city, where my father now worked as an independent electrician.

I shared a pleasant enough room with Felice, but of course I had to have a studio. The only place was in the attic of our apartment. It was very hot and there were nests of rats between the walls. When I was out of the room, the rats would emerge. I was terrified of them and before I opened the door, I would bang on it wildly to scare the rats back between the walls.

It wasn't a very nice place to be, but it was my own. I could be absolutely alone to do what I wanted, and what I wanted to do was sculpt. In spite of the fact that I had had only the most basic instruction, I decided to begin a life-sized work. I knew it would be useless to try to persuade anyone to come up to my sweltering little attic to sit for me; so I pulled my table and materials directly in front of my mirror and used myself as a model.

As I worked, I forgot about time and the heat and the perspiration soaking my skin. I seemed to exist only as eyes and fingers and a terrible force that willed to bring out of the clay the girl I saw in the mirror. I often forgot that the model was myself.

At the sanatorium where I was teaching gymnastics, I met a woman doctor who had married a very famous painter. Later in life he was to become head of the Art Academy in Budapest. He wanted to do an oil of a young woman and asked me to sit for him. Later he was to sell the painting for an enormous sum of money, but while he was working on it he liked to joke and call us both *dilettantes*, me with my sculpting and him with his painting.

27

One day he decided to see my sculpting for himself; so he came to our flat in the city and followed me up the attic stairs to my little loft, laughing as I pounded on the door to scare the rats, bowing grandly to me as he stooped to enter the room. I was in an agony of excitement. I could feel my heart pounding against my ribs. My hands were ice cold. My artist friend walked slowly around the sculpture.

Suddenly I felt ashamed. I wanted to throw a cloth over the image of myself sitting so solidly and so stupidly on the table. I stared at his face. It seemed he would never speak. He raised my window shade and walked around the sculpture again. I stood in the doorway wishing I could flee down the stairs, out of the apartment, through the streets of our city and all the way back to Vienna. Finally he stood still and glanced quickly at me as if he had just remembered that I was there. He pulled me into the room and laughed at my tense face.

"You have a wonderful talent, little Rose!"

I stared at him. Was he making fun? I turned to the sculpture on the table that had filled me with such self-loathing. It looked vulnerable and small.

"I mean it! You are gifted! Rose, Rose!" He shook me a little until I smiled. I began to feel a little hot. I sat down on my bed. He continued talking, running his hands lightly over the sculpting as he spoke.

"You cannot stay here and work by yourself. If you want to be a sculptor, you must have a teacher. You must work with other artists and learn from the beginning."

A great joy began to fill me. "You *like* it?"

With a grin he pulled me up from the bed and down the stairs, talking excitedly as we clattered into the cool shade of the street.

"If you want to continue sculpting, I have a friend, a famous sculptor in Budapest. He has his own studio and he will take you as a student if I ask him. You will have to give your life to this, Rose, to the study of art, to the discipline of the apprentice. It may take years, but you will not be alone. You will be with a master sculptor, and you yourself will become a great artist."

I felt as if I were in a dream. I could see that we were now entering the vast park that separated Piešťany from the city. Soon we would be crossing the bridge. We passed the little cafes with their orchestras. They all seemed to be playing dances. I wanted to fling myself into the air in ecstasy. What he was saying was too good to be true. He liked what I had done! I could become a famous sculptor!

But something he was saying hit me with a terrible pain. I stopped on the path in dismay.

"Of course you must give up your dancing!" he repeated. "Art will take everything. All your energies, all your talent must be poured into it. You cannot divide yourself and become great. That is the only condition."

For days I was torn. I stared at my hands. They felt filled with the assurance of power and seemed to move of themselves, touching, stroking, grasping a cup, the smoothness of the side of a chair, the knotted muscles at the back of my neck, the curve of a spoon. I ached with the need within me to give them liberty, to free them to pound and pull and carve out of nothing the beauty that filled the thousand things of creation. But to abandon the dance! That was a denial of my whole body, all that I had learned and loved in Vienna, music and liberty and my very soul.

My family counseled me in the calm of common sense. Sculpting was plainly a more reasonable pursuit than the dance. After all, what is created in sculpting endures and can even be sold, and does not die away with the last notes of music or the coming of old age.

Felice pointed out that in Budapest I would be close to home, and I could even support myself there with the help of an uncle who was a doctor in the Health Ministry. He could urge his friends who were doctors to send patients in need of physiotherapy to me. I could put to good use my gymnastic training and what I had learned that summer in the sanatorium at Piešťany.

And so it was that I decided to become a sculptor. When the season ended, I traveled to Budapest to begin a new life there. It was to be the beginning of my sorrows.

III

The Flood

I HAD BEEN TO BUDAPEST many times in my childhood during the difficult war years. But now Budapest was a peacetime city and I was a young woman. We both had come to new strength and liberty. I felt it as I glided down the hilly streets of Budapest, squinting my eyes against the hot autumn sun to see my favorite fort on the grassy slopes of Castle Hill.

A different spirit had taken over the city. All the old ways of life seemed to have fallen away. Everything new and all opposites and all paradoxes were adored. There was a feeling of something having been set in motion. People talked about new art—a new man—new ways of thinking. Destruction and creation dimmed and flashed like opposite sides of a dangling moon, and people were hypnotized and fascinated and exhilarated and confused. Everyone made of life what he liked.

For me all possibilities beckoned, opportunities unraveled like a ball of string. There was nothing I couldn't do, and I had chosen to study art and become a famous sculptor. I had youth and talent, and my friends thought I was beautiful.

I found a place to board with a middle-class elderly Jewish couple whom I came to love. Their daughter, Helen, and her husband were both journalists, and through them I drifted easily into the inner circles of Budapest's artistic and intellectual life.

But in the beginning it was Herr Pátzay, the famous sculptor who had consented to be my teacher, who filled my every working thought with dread and a terrible determination to win his praise. He was a man of long silences, with eyes so piercing they seemed to cut through the marble he worked on. Often as I watched him tap and chip and chisel, I found myself half thinking it was his eyes and not the sharp points of his tools that cut away the stone so masterfully.

His method of teaching me was to slap a mass of wet clay on my modeling stand and walk away. As I wedged and pushed and squeezed the clay, he would mock my clumsiness, my slowness, insisting that there were air bubbles in the clay when there were not, inquiring with elaborate politeness if I thought I was making bread. Whatever I did aroused his sarcasm. Frequently his scathing comments contained elements of instruction, and so in this way I could glean direction. Perhaps hours would pass in silence, the only sounds in the studio the pushing of his chisel back and forth over the marble or the rasping sound of a tool being sharpened on his grindstone, and the slapping, pulling, pounding of my hands as I free-modeled the clay. Often at the end of the day when my clay was leathery and I thought beautifully formed, Herr Pátzay would suddenly appear at my shoulder and scoff at all that I had done as being without design, rhythm, proportion, or any element of art.

To Herr Pátzay, drawing was very important. It was the means, he said, of capturing the fleeting beauty of movement and gesture for later use in sculpting. If my work in clay was trifling, my drawing was beneath contempt and he decided that I must enroll in an art school and learn to draw. I had always been a poor artist, and I knew even then that the power in my hands was to form in clay or plaster or stone and not to use a brush or pencil to express my inner spirit. But I was far too afraid of my teacher to refuse.

I soon discovered there was a great deal to the study of art. There were the classes in theory where we studied what I thought to be tiresome concepts—the function of the line, the interrelation of line with light, color, space, contour, mass, shadow.

There were long hours bent over my sketch pad, shading, erasing, practicing basic cubic and cylindrical forms. But happily we students were also expected to become familiar with the great painters whose works hung in the galleries of Budapest. Once again I felt free, transported by the beauty of the ancient city and the grandeur of the works of Botticelli, Leonardo, Raphael, Titian, Dürer, Rembrandt, Vermeer. Often I was strangely moved by the religious themes of so many of the greatest paintings. We studied modern Hungarian painters—Pogany, Glatz, Csok—and for the first time the glory of the artist's vision of color and movement and drama and meaning swept through my soul.

In that heightened consciousness I felt terribly alive, open to new ideas, experiences, knowledge. It seemed that everyone I met, my journalists, my artists, my teachers, my student friends, overflowed with all that was different and strange and wonderfully, profoundly important.

People spoke of Nietzsche's brilliance and of his philosophy of the man who through superior integrity, courage, and creative will has surpassed in the power of sublimation. A faint faraway bell began to chime. Nietzsche called this surpassing man the superman whom each cycle of life seeks as the hope toward its fulfillment. There would be a cataclysm that would destroy all that would impede the way to the possible realization of what a victory might be. This he conceived as "joyous tragedy."

Helen, my landlady's daughter, worked on a Budapest newspaper and had taken me under her wing. She had lovely expressive eyes that shone as she talked, explaining, opening up, discussing the ideas I brought to her—notions, systems of thought, slogans, doctrines that flowed in the early thirties through the air of Budapest almost as tangibly as the lazy Danube that cut a watery path through the center of our city.

I asked her about Nietzsche's declaration that it is a sign of weakness in an artist to be concerned with the moral aspect of his art. And about his severity against distinctions of good and evil, which he said were not constants but functional values.

For reasons I was soon to understand, Helen was not a devotee of Nietzsche, but she was not at all distressed by what he wrote. Her view was that ignorance was the cause of evil and that certain knowledge would overcome evil; there would then be a triumph of release.

Sometimes we discussed the toxic currents of anti-Semitism that streamed out of the political turmoil in Germany, inflaming, smoldering infectious pockets of fanaticism in the intellectual life of Europe. As a journalist, Helen closely followed politics. She pressed her hands together and shook her head in exasperation as she discussed the new German movement, National Socialism, led by a fanatical nationalist, Adolf Hitler. Helen was one of only a very few people in Hungary who had bothered to read Hitler's book, *Mein Kampf* (My Struggle), and even she had only read part of it. Once in a while she would recite anti-Semitic quotes from it to document her assertion (which was commonly held by everyone we knew in Budapest) that Hitler was a lunatic.

"The National Socialist movement must call eternal wrath upon the head of the foul enemy of mankind, the inexorable Jew."

"Hence today I believe that I am acting in accordance with the will of the Almighty Creator: By defending myself against the Jew, I am fighting for the work of the Lord."

"Marriage must be raised from the level of continuous defilement of the race and be given the consecration of an institution which is called upon to produce images of the Lord and no monstrosities halfway between man and ape [Gentile and Jew]."

Helen was convinced that any enlightened man would readily understand Hitler's ideas for what they were—twisted and absurd. As his statements became more widely known, they would be flung away in the light of day and in the pure air of reason. The rantings of this madman would soon become only a demented whisper in the back streets and alleys of Germany where malcontents huddled and nursed their festering delusions.

Einstein's theory of relativity had just been made known, and in Budapest we spent hours in the cafes discussing its ramifications. We agreed that the basis of a work of art is one's point of view about life and the universe, but now that space and time had been invested with new dimensions, what effect would this knowledge have on creativity?

Helen and her husband belonged to a select group of intellectuals and artists, some eccentric to my point of view, called

"Gnostics." They were examining relativity at their meetings, and Helen invited me to attend.

At first I understood nothing. Eclectic discussions seemed to have been already going on for hours when we arrived, and the first evening was spent in talking, smoking, talking until long past midnight. For a while I was excited to be included in such an inner circle, and I observed the intense conversation with a face I hoped I had arranged in a perceptive and teachable expression.

Eventually I began to understand that it was "spirit" that everyone thought to be important. I learned that the human being has not only a body and a soul, but also a spirit. I was electrified. I had never thought about spirit.

A young journalist friend of Helen's, Louis, attended the meetings. I thought him unattractive and faintly unpleasant, but he enjoyed explaining words to me that I did not understand. Many in the group had New Testaments and could quote from these writings. Louis said that the teaching of Gnosticism was an ancient wisdom from the Scriptures, and it was given to only a few to understand it. It was secret wisdom.

Often the discussions would go on so late that I would become desperately sleepy. At such time I would curl up on a couch somewhere and take a nap. When I sat up and stretched, there Louis would be waiting, ready to sit beside me and continue my initiation.

"The world is ruled by evil *archons*," he would say. "Jehovah in the Bible is one of these." Since Louis was a Jew and knew Scriptures well, I supposed he knew what he was talking about, even though I was sure that my mother had never prayed to an evil *archon* in her quiet hours by the river with her prayer book.

"These *archons* hold captive the spirit of man. Jesus Christ was a being called an *aeon* sent from the heavenly *pleroma* to restore the lost knowledge of man's divine origin."

If I yawned or appeared confused, Louis would jump up and bring me coffee with cream or little cakes with tea. Soon I became aware that it was not only religious zeal that motivated Louis. His interest in me went beyond that of only the human spirit, and I began to find him troublesome even though I was flattered by his attentions.

I noticed there was an aspect of our modern Hungarian Gnosticism that had to do with the "surpassing man," that within our secret knowledge was the potential for a higher, privileged human with superior powers.

One of our main teachers was a man who would eat no food that had been cooked. Everything had to be raw, and he claimed that he would live 10,000 years on earth. (Actually he was to die at age seventy.)

"Mankind is divided into flesh, soul, and spirit," this man would teach, the bony fingers of one of his hands counting out the divisions of mankind on the other. "Mankind is also partitioned into classes representing each of these elements. A person who is merely a body lacks spirit and can never be saved." I shuddered at the idea. What if I were such a person? I didn't think so. Always in the deepest parts of my soul, like a melody or a memory one can't quite remember, was a sadness, a longing I could not define, a homesickness, but for no place I had ever been. In German the word for this state of being is *Sehnsucht*. Surely I at least had a soul!

"We Gnostics bear the knowledge of the divine spark or spirit, and our salvation is certain." But was *I* really a Gnostic?

"It is possible that devout Christians and some others might attain a lesser kind of salvation, even in their ignorance, through faith."

I reflected that as a Jew I would have to attain the "sure salvation" our teacher described through the secret knowledge of Gnosticism. I didn't want a "lesser" salvation anyway, and I liked the teaching that our bodies were quite indifferent entities in the matter of salvation. What we did with them or did not do was of little importance. It was the secret, higher wisdom that was of supreme importance. How useless to beat the body, to starve it, to torture it with lack of sleep or exercise as I had seen some Catholics do in Pieš'tany. How ignorant and terrible the ancient whipping block under the cross! With all my heart I pitied people who endured such agonies.

Another of the teachers was a woman from the countryside near Budapest who was also a vegetarian and who taught that we must deny our bodies nothing except the expression of violence. She stressed the importance of imitating Jesus who was a great teacher who had come into the world to bring love. Jesus never fought back and pacifism, she said, ought to be the life-aim of enlightened man. Louis often read me passages from the New Testament that contained Jesus' words and urged me to enter ever more deeply into the teachings.

Louis soon began to be a major part of my life. I was surprised when he first began to frequent my studio, waiting for me to be finished. Often, after a long severe day, he would make me laugh and praise my beauty and talent and ask me to dance for him. After the tension and frustration of hours with Herr Pátzay, Louis cheered me up. Eventually he enrolled at the school where I had night classes in art, professing the desire to paint as well as to express himself in his job as a journalist, an occupation he declared limited his creativity.

It became quickly evident that he was a hopeless artist, but he ignored his failures and continued with his lessons, saying he had to be with me. Late at night he would walk me home through the deserted streets of Budapest, coming into my boarding house for coffee. Since he was a friend of Helen and her parents, and a part of our Gnostic group, I could not discourage his night visits to the house.

Yet there was something in Louis that repelled me, even though he seemed to have a profound knowledge about mystical things. I thought he must be one of the high spirits we talked about, higher than most people, and I was paradoxically flattered by his intense attraction to me. Everywhere I turned, there Louis seemed to be, devouring me with his enormous dark eyes, noting what gave me pleasure, soothing all my stormy moods, celebrating my joys and small triumphs.

So he began to court me in earnest. When summer came, I agreed that he could visit me in Piešťany. I ought to have been warned by the shocked disappointment of my family, but in my headstrong way I defended Louis against their disapproval. If they thought him arrogant, I declared he was brilliant. If they pointed out his irresponsibility and extravagance, I defended his interest in the higher things of the mind over materialistic concerns. My sister Felice, now herself a glowing new bride, tried to like Louis for my sake, but I could sense her anxiety in the way she watched Louis and me together.

When we returned to Budapest, Louis was determined that we

37

would marry even though he felt keenly the reservations of my family. By this time I was very deeply involved with him and he was untiringly persistent. So I gave in and we were married.

Often I had told my friends that if I were not famous before I was forty, I would kill myself; and when I said it, I truly meant it. It would have been inconceivable to me to imagine that marriage would ever touch in any way my aspirations to become a great sculptor. I would continue my studies with Herr Pátzay, contributing to our livelihood when I could by taking on physiotherapy patients. Louis would support us with his rather indifferent newspaper work, which even so was adequate for the needs of a young couple.

In the very early days, in spite of the political chaos around us, the world seemed to be at my feet. Louis declared himself to be the happiest man in the world. I convinced myself that I was deliriously happy and threw myself into sculpting with renewed dedication. Once in a while Herr Pátzay would give me a word of grudging praise, and I knew that it would not be only Rose, now, who would be a famous sculptor. It would also be Louis' wife! Louis had a strange and tremendous power over me, in spite of my strong will. Soon I was to learn the source of his compelling influence.

One night when Louis came home from his work at the paper, he presented me with an invitation for us to visit his cousin, Max, who lived in the country. I had never met his cousin and in those days, in Budapest, everyone loved to get out of the city on weekends and into the forests and hills to commune with nature. Eagerly I agreed. Louis told me I would like his cousin. He was a very deep person who studied psychic phenomena and had been given many gifts of wisdom. I was intrigued.

It was wonderful to escape Budapest and the political tension that hung over the city like an oppressive heat wave. In Budapest, people seemed increasingly frenzied—working too hard, drinking too much, laughing too loudly, arguing vehemently. There were terrible rumors that people refused to believe, but the rumors were sought out with a fascination that was part of the sickness of those times. It was said that in Germany, jails were so full that the National Socialists were building prison camps for thousands of political prisoners and Jews. We had seen photographs of boarded-up German/Jewish shops, and heard it was no longer possible for Jews to be teachers in Germany or hold important jobs in the professions and civil services. To Louis and me, what was happening in Germany seemed faraway and unreal. Our lives were just starting and we had our destiny to fulfill. Like many young people of our country, we tried to shut our eyes and think about other things. Perhaps that is why the occult became so popular. It was a way of shutting out the confusion of the times, of gaining power in a world I wanted to conquer and rule, a world that was betraying me by its own disintegration and despair.

There were a lot of people at Max's house that weekend. Perhaps we all were playing roles that we disbelieved. I for one was the radiant bride, fearless, independent, the soon-to-be-famous sculptress. Not exactly an intellectual but certainly a pseudo-genius, showing off with my fluency in several languages, my spontaneous bursts of dance. When I talked I used my hands and arms as expressively as I could, hoping people would constantly be reminded that these were the hands of a brilliant sculptress. Louis was proud of me and bragged about my achievements as well as his own. We all boasted and laughed and tried to create a world of our own, the way we wanted it to be. We tried to believe we were the real and important people who lived in it.

But when it came time for Max's seance, a strangeness fell over the group. We felt different, quieter, deeper, as if we could now leave our frivolous selves and enter into a world so apart from our own there was no longer need for pretense and pride. We approached the spirits humbly, willing to learn of them. We were eager to utterly abandon ourselves to this world we could not see or touch, dependent on the willingness of the spirits to reveal themselves.

I could sense an oddness in the atmosphere of the room. Max drew the heavy curtains shut, making the room almost black except for the sputtering of a few small candles on the fireplace mantel. Our chairs were pulled into a circle, and we sat reverently in the presence of spirits we hoped to contact. Max astonished me by an immediate trance and began speaking in a wavery voice of "the other side" and the things that were there. I was thrilled at his descriptions of peace and beauty, sounds and sights that equaled and mirrored the loveliest on earth, but always superior in some way. But soon Max's voice seemed to fade away into faint weeping which became louder. The room was full of many voices, sobbing, moaning in the most heartbroken way. I was appalled at the sound of so much grief.

The spirits seemed to gather around my head, and my heart was wrung with compassion for them. "Why are you weeping?" It seemed as natural to ask as one would ask a child.

They called themselves "airing spirits" and begged for help. They said they didn't know who they were or where and they were terribly unhappy. I tried to explain to them that they were spirits, that they were dead, and that they belonged in the beautiful world Max had been describing to us. They seemed comforted. They asked if they might go there. I assured them and seemed, one by one, to be dismissing them into that place of peace. When I had finished, there was silence in the room.

Max tiptoed to the window and pulled open the drapes. Twilight was falling and the room remained dim. Max and Louis and everyone in the group were gazing at me with admiration. What had *I* done? I stared back in bewilderment. Finally Louis got up and came over to my chair. He bent and kissed me softly. "Rose, my dearest, you are a medium!" His voice was tender with awe. I was pleased to have discovered another of my talents.

When Louis and I returned to Budapest after our weekend in the country, I was restless and felt strangely anxious about my work in sculpting. I was determined to be a great sculptor, but success and recognition seemed to be taking too long. I began to have a sense of urgency. Conditions in Europe were growing increasingly tense. Nation after nation was arming, in spite of alliances, peace agreements, treaties. Europe was like a drum with the skin stretched to the splitting point. An inexorable, muffled battle beat throbbed in the air.

In depression-torn Germany, the fanatic we in Budapest had laughed at had achieved hysterical popularity. On January 30, 1933, Paul von Hindenburg, the president of the fragmented German Republic, administered the oath of office to Adolf Hitler, whom he had decided just the day before to make Chancellor. Our Hungarian papers were full of the story. Hitler had sworn, "I will employ my strength for the welfare of the German people, protect the Constitution and laws of the German people, conscientiously discharge the duties imposed on me, and conduct my affairs of office impartially and with justice to everyone."

But even as Hitler was taking the oath, frenzied crowds packed the streets of Germany celebrating the event by shouting the Nazi slogan, *"Deutschland erwache, Juda verrecke"* (Germany awake, Death to the Jews). It was a German dogma that Jews controlled the Republic and had brought upon the German peoples the sufferings and losses of the war and the Great Depression. Hitler preached that the professions and trades were controlled by Jews. Worst of all was what he called the "Jew press." Jews, he insisted, were the masters of the German press and had to be removed. (Louis retorted hotly that out of the top 100 papers in Germany, only ten were edited by Jews.) Jews, Hitler said, controlled the banks and were making themselves wealthy at the expense of the poverty and unemployment of the German people. In Germany, disillusionment was entrenched. People were looking for a Messiah to rescue them from their misfortunes. With Hitler came the mass ideology of *blut* and *rasse* (blood and race), and with this new god was created a new devil, the Jew, source of all German evils, who lived among the Aryans but who was of a different race and blood.

Delirious anti-Semitism reverberated throughout Europe, dinning reason and arousing ancient suspicions, jealousies, fears. In our own Budapest lived half of all the Jews in Hungary. We were 20 percent of the population, mostly in the cultured, professional strata of the city. Many Jews were actually baptized Christians—perhaps throughout Hungary there were as many as 35,000. From the mid-twenties until Hitler, times had been good for Jews in Hungary under the impartial leadership of our prime minister, Count Stephen Bethlen.

But now as the thirties progressed, the odd spirit I had sensed when I first came to Budapest—the change, the thrill of contradiction, absurdity, new ways of thinking—became a dark swirling of disruption, a foreboding of ruin. Music seemed louder, dissonant laughter raucous, ambition obsessive.

Or was my growing anxiety simply a symptom of a strangeness in Louis, an unevenness in our relationship that I tried to ignore or minimize? It began with what I at first had thought was a sweet grudging of the time I spent at the studio or my art classes. Louis had lost interest in attending art school and complained that I ought to be spending my evenings with him and not working. He began to say that if I loved him I would give up art, since art was not really a part of his world and he could not share it with me. If I loved him, I would not shut him out of so much of my existence. If I truly loved him, I would throw my life away for him if he asked it. And all he was asking was that I give him a little of my time.

At first I teased him about being silly, but as his harassment grew, so did my determination to resist what he was asking of me. I had been willful all my life, and his attempts to force me to give up everything for him brought out the fierce stubbornness of my nature. Sculpting was my lifeblood, the soul and spirit of me. Perhaps I even sculpted better because Louis objected.

I dreamed of his relenting when I became famous. How proud he would be of his wife and the fortune I would make! Already I was someone to be taken notice of in artistic circles in Budapest. But in time! Louis would come to see he had been wrong in trying to stop me.

Sometimes when I came home from the studio or from working with one of my well-paying physiotherapy patients, Louis would be drunk, saying he had nothing better to do with his time. I was deeply shocked because drunkenness is uncommon in the Jewish community. But there were worse shocks to come!

One day I was at home scrubbing the floor of our small apartment, then hanging some new prints I had bought from a friend who painted in a cafe in our neighborhood. Louis was at home, sipping coffee and admiring the "domestic" Rose. Casually I asked Louis where he had been the night before when I was working. A strange smile passed over his face. He shrugged, "I was amusing myself with some women. What do you think men do in their spare time?"

Casual sexual alliances were common in our circles. My own philosophical readings had made conventional morality a matter of theoretical indifference to me. My own young adult life was an example of unrestrained self-pleasing. I had lived for art, done as I pleased, and judged no one. But I was not a real Bohemian at heart. And my ideas of married loyalty had been steadfastly fixed in the lovely Eden of Piešťany and the devotion of my parents to each other. Promiscuity was a horrifying betrayal.

Louis laughed in astonishment at my reaction. He suddenly seemed to find pleasure in taunting me. He had been unfaithful to me since the early days of our marriage. Surely I knew and didn't care! Why was I suddenly pretending to be so offended? He began naming names, describing scenes. It was unbearable.

I ran weeping out of our apartment. The buildings and people I passed on the streets were blurred and seemed faraway. I felt my spirit strangling inside of me. I was suffocating with shock and shame. I don't remember how many hours I spent wandering the streets. When I returned home, I staggered with fatigue and spent emotion. Louis was alarmed. He tried to comfort me. He promised he would give up these other women. They meant nothing to him. I was the only one he loved. He stroked my hair and washed my face as if I were a little child. But his words meant nothing.

I became desperately unhappy. Soon I began going again to spiritualist meetings, hoping for some meaning to the emotional chaos in which I lived. My disgust and brokenheartedness at Louis's behavior only seemed to make him pursue women more wantonly, enjoying my despair. Night after night he would confess to me and promise not to continue. I begged him not to tell me, to let me try to continue my sculpting. Our life together became grotesque. Black and ruinous images filled my mind.

When summer came I returned home to Piešťany without Louis. All spring I had had a fever. I was sleepless and sometimes sat hopelessly weeping for hours. Louis grew furious with my depression and spent our money wildly, sometimes all of it in the same day. Many nights he would come home and describe what girl he had been with. I would rush blindly out of the apartment, unable to bear the humiliation.

Sometimes he would beg my forgiveness and promise never to hurt me again, telling me I was too good for him, too talented, too beautiful, and if I would love him again, he would completely reform. If I could not love him, he declared, he would never let me go anyway because he needed me in order to live.

We went quite often, even in those terrible days, to the Gnos-

43

tic meetings and to spiritualist meetings, but there was no relief in any of them for me. Louis often gave talks, and there were times when he lectured that I thought that he was much higher than I—that his thinking was on such an elevated plane that it was I who was wrong and didn't understand such genius and how such a person had to live. It was I who was making his life miserable. It was I who was to blame for the misery of our existence.

By the summertime when I arrived in Piešťany, I was suffering terribly. My family could see I was desperately unhappy. Felice was now the proud mother of twin baby boys and even though she had maids and a nurse for the babies, I stayed with her and her husband to "help" her with the children and to rest at the hotel where her husband was the manager. After a while the peace and beauty of Piešťany restored me a little, and I began to sleep again and to be able to take walks and speak without weeping. Felice begged me to divorce Louis, but I felt bound to him. Often he would telephone and persuade me that everything would be different if at the end of the summer I would return to him in Budapest.

When I did, I discovered that Louis was deeply in debt. He was unconcerned and felt we could easily pay what we owed once I began working again as a physiotherapist. It was only a matter of days before I realized that coming back to him had been folly. Louis had never intended to be faithful, and he continued to take feverish pleasure in confessing his sexual affairs to me in detail. So we began a destructive cycle: I would leave Louis, then he would persuade me to return; yet each reunion was destroyed by ever more cruel and sadistic behavior. Sometimes he wrote poems about our life and how he created an inferno that was to swallow us up in a cosmic disaster. Sculpting became impossible.

Finally I knew I had to get away where he could not pursue me. The ludicrous idea came to me to escape as a domestic servant to another country. Through an agency in Budapest, I was actually hired by a titled family in England, who would pay my fare to Britain and give me an allowance in exchange for my work for them. I was so despondent I cared nothing about what I did or where I went. I wanted only to get out of Budapest and as far away from Louis as possible. I had thought that I would be in London and working in a household with only three people, but instead I was sent to the country estate of a noble family where large numbers of people came often for hunting and dinner. I was taken as the first parlor maid. The second parlor maid was a Hungarian girl whose name was also Rose. In order to minimize confusion, I was given the English name of Mary.

It was a time of high patriotism and optimism in England, and everything English was valued and loved. Shy King George VI had just been crowned after the abdication of his brother, Edward VIII. Although the family for which I worked could speak French fluently, as could I, they took great pains to speak only English to me and to teach me their language and the customs of their great country. In an honored position on the walls of the manor were beautifully framed paintings of the King and Queen of England and their two tiny daughters, Elizabeth and Margaret Rose.

In Hungarian we have an expression, "To fall from the pail into the bucket," and if I was wretched when I arrived in England, I was soon to learn that my misery would intensify. On the first morning in the household, I was given a printed list of what I was expected to do every five minutes from 6:30 A.M. to 11 P.M. at night. Each week I had half a day off and a whole day off once a month.

Sixteen and a half hours of work a day, six and a half days a week— and I had thought I would be able to see England! I wanted to study the English language in my spare time and perhaps go on to travel to Paris on days off, maybe saving enough money to visit my brothers in far-off America!

It was beyond even my wild Hungarian imagination to conceive an existence as confined as an English parlor maid! To have the day divided into minutes and to give account for every one of them seemed outrageous at first. But even more intolerable for me was the cold, impersonal way servants were treated. There were no "first slices of meat for the maid" in England! It was not even permitted for servants to say "good morning" when the Master or Lady first appeared in the day. One had to wait until one was first spoken to or remain silent. Every detail of life was so precise and so restrained, I felt my very soul had been taken out of me and returned starched as stiffly as the rustling white apron I wore.

In the household, servants could make no noise, show no emotion, have no conversation except as it pertained to duties in all the long working day. The exceptions were meals and tea breaks. At those times, the English servants commented disparagingly on the "foreign help" and corrected our speech and ideas. I became silent, struggling with my emotions and the bland English food that sickened me; the sticky porridge and overcooked vegetables and the sweet slippery puddings that turned to mush in my mouth.

Often I would sob hopelessly in my bed throughout the black country nights. My life had lost form and definition. It was like a wet watercolor when the paints run together and ruin the picture. I was a dancer, a sculptor, accustomed to praise, excitement, artistic achievement, expression. I was a married woman from a large, loving family.

Yet I had imprisoned myself in this lonely, cold land where people spoke their difficult language in deadly quiet and permitted no laughter and no music and no warmth. What was the point of pouring out my life and strength in carrying trays and cleaning rooms and serving meals? Did I not say I would be famous before I was forty or die? Was I the Rose of Vienna and Budapest, bursting with life and talent and promise? Was I the despised wife of Louis, humiliated and disgraced? Had I become nothing more than the English "Mary," good for only the "Yes, your Ladyships" of the drawing room and parlors?

Perhaps her Ladyship became concerned over my despondency. One day she took me on an unprecedented outing to a neighboring city. She had shopping to do and while she was busy, she directed me to spend the time becoming acquainted with young people at the town's YWCA hall. I am sure the utter incongruity of the visit of a Hungarian Jewess, artist, parlor maid to an English YWCA meeting was quite lost on her Ladyship. She left me with a satisfied smile, assuring me I would quite enjoy a little change.

I stood awkwardly in the plain lobby of the small building. There was a thin carpet in the middle of the floor and a towering aspidistra in one of the room's corners. An assortment of sagging chairs lined the walls.

As it happened, there were two English secretaries at the Y

that afternoon who spoke a little German, and we became acquainted. The girls were charming and simple in a polite English way, and I think they felt it their duty to be kind to a stranger who had the added misfortune of not being English.

They were waiting to attend a religious meeting to which they invited me to come. I had had meetings enough in Budapest, with the Gnostics and the spiritualists, but there was nothing else to do. We entered a small side room and joined a few others sitting on straight wooden chairs. For a few moments everyone was silent. Then a whitehaired woman began singing a hymn; the others joined in and more hymns followed. They did not sing well, those few English people who were gathered there, but as the hymns wavered in the air and grew stronger, a longing filled my soul until I thought I would burst with grief and despair. Suddenly there was silence again. People appeared to be meditating. I wondered if they were calling forth spirits, but no one spoke. After a long time, a man rose to read a few verses from the New Testament. People sat again for a long time and then one by one began to get up and leave, some glancing at me with discreet curiosity. My two new friends introduced me to the man who had read the Scriptures. I later learned that it was not customary for English people to make friends quickly with strangers, but the man was very kind to me and invited me and the two secretaries to his home for tea the following week on my half-day off.

When her Ladyship picked me up after her shopping, she was pleased at my social success. She smiled absently when I reported that I had been asked to tea in the home of the religious speaker.

It was a proper English tea that graced the table of the kindly couple who had invited us girls to their small home. I discovered that the man was an engineer, a genteel middle-class Englishman who wore a suitcoat and vest and tie for tea. He and his wife greeted us with the restrained courtesy of the English and sat us down to a table of jams, buttered bread, and meat pastries. Cups of steaming tea issued from a generous brown teapot. We ate daintily as we chatted. For dessert there was a pudding and two kinds of cake. The homey atmosphere was in such contrast to the museum-like splendor of my place of employment, I relaxed for the first time in England.

It seemed natural to ask about the meeting I had attended the week before. It was very difficult for me to understand the man's explanations of his religious practices. He spoke of man's "inner light," and gave me a little booklet which he thought would describe what he meant better than he could say it himself. I wanted to understand, but even when I studied his booklet in the candlelight of my tiny room in the top of the house, I could make no sense out of it. My mind returned to the yearnings of the Budapest Gnostics for the higher secret knowledge. Was this a higher knowledge? But how then could it be *within* man? Such knowledge had to come from the outside of man, from the *aeons*. And what of the spirit world? Perhaps the inner light actually came from spirits like the ones I had communicated with in Budapest at the seance at Max's house. As I reflected on this idea of inner light, I remembered my childhood Sabbaths at Aunt Caroline's home, the flickering of the candles, the prayers about light:

> *Blessed art Thou, O Lord our God, King of the Universe, who at Thy word bringest on the evening twilight, with wisdom openest the gates of the heavens, and with understanding changest times and variest the seasons, and arranges the stars in their watches in the sky, according to Thy will. Thou createst day and night; Thou rollest away the light from before the darkness; Thou rollest away the light from before the darkness. . . .*

The words burned into my soul. I could feel my own darkness thickening inside me, a black, dead mood that gripped me as I worked through the long hours of that cold English summer. Hour by hour my will loosened its hold on life, and I longed for release from the heartache that weighted my every breath.

I knew that all my dreams were over. I would not be a great dancer. Never again would my hands sculpt. I would never attain the fame and fortune that once seemed my inevitable destiny. The failure of my marriage filled me with shame and disgust. I could not return to Europe, to Budapest, to Louis. I could not face my family at Piešťany. But to stay in English service, every moment of my life spent in submissive labor, ignored, unloved, without music or art or freedom, was intolerable.

One day I felt I could stand it no longer, and I began to weep in the kitchen, telling the cook I wanted to run away, to leave the family, to get out of service. The cook went immediately to her Ladyship and reported what I had said. After that, all human civility toward me ceased. Her Ladyship was angry and told me I was bound by English law to work in her household because she had paid my travel expenses from Hungary, and I myself had signed an agreement.

From that time on, I was treated as an outcast by all the members of the household. My few privileges were cut off. I tried to see my friends at the YWCA, but her Ladyship refused to permit me to use the telephone. My letters home were removed from the mail packet that was sent every day to the village post. Everyone found fault with every job I did, and when there was not sarcastic criticism, there was frigid silence.

Louis had persuaded my gentle mother to give him my address. His letters were impassioned, begging me to return to him, declaring he would never let me go and at the same time telling me about one or another of the women with whom he was staying.

I began to plan my death. I had some jewelry that was worth something, and one day I managed to get to the city and gave it to one of the English girls I knew. She became very frightened, and after I returned to the household she got a message to me begging me to go to the home of the Manager of the Labor Exchange in the town.

I had already cut ties with life, and I felt myself drifting easily into oblivion. Nothing at all mattered, and it was of no consequence to me if I went to see this man or not. But my friend's note was so urgent, something in it moved me out of the house in the middle of the day and across the countryside to the city where the man lived.

After walking trance-like over the lush green of the English fields, I came upon a road. As I followed it, I felt utterly detached from the blue of the sky over my head and the sound of birds and the rustle of small creatures on the roadside as I passed. The sun on my back did not warm me. A bus braked slowly to a stop beside me. "Get in, love," the driver invited, and as I had followed my friend's request I obeyed the driver. The bus was going to the Labor Manager's city.

Somehow after a time I found myself at his house. With

complete indifference I raised the knocker bar that hung over the post slot on the middle of his front door. In an instant, the door was flung open and in that movement I was rescued.

Never had simple kindness and understanding meant so much to me. The Manager's wife instantly understood my despair and took me into her heart as if I were her daughter. There was no question of my returning to her Ladyship. I was to stay with them. I was to rest. I was to eat. I was to leave everything to the Labor Manager and he would work it out. Blurred days passed into weeks, and I began to see the shining of the sun and to agree with myself to live a little longer.

Increasingly I wanted to see my mother, and I asked about arrangements to go home. The Manager understood my home-sickness, but he and his wife were determined that I should not return to the Continent. His efforts to keep me in England amazed me. He worked with a ferocity I found inexplicable. If he had obtained permission for me to remain in England I would have agreed, so great was my dread of Louis and my fear of returning to a life of marital anguish in Budapest. But in the end the Manager came to me in distress and said I would have to return home.

It is strange that in those days, when I knew thousands of Jews were fleeing Europe, when in Palestine Jewish organizations were fighting both the British quotas and the Arabs to help Jews enter the land, I gave so little thought to any danger. I was far more fearful of Louis than I was of Hitler. My ruined career, the disgrace of my failed marriage obsessed me.

The Manager tried to prepare me by describing the situation in Europe. It was very bad. All countries were massing immense armies in the name of peace. Shocking stories had been confirmed about the actual persecution of Jews in Germany. Open anti-Jewish legislation in the Third Reich had increased to such intensity that Jews were brutally humiliated, discharged from their jobs and professions, their businesses and homes confiscated.

Hitler had come to power in 1933. Now, only five years later, there were only two principles in all of Germany: rule by führer-ship, and the domination of race.

I suppose I responded to the inevitable by assuring the Labor Manager and his wife that things were altogether different in

Hungary. We in Budapest felt German politics unrelated to us and we were not only allies of Germany, but well protected by our government. It would have been closer to the truth to tell this kind English couple that I didn't really care what happened to me. How could they know how completely I felt my life to be over?

On the day of my departure, I remember the Manager's wife looking repeatedly at my train ticket to Vienna as if I were in danger of being taken straight to Germany. "If only you could stay here!" My shunting train eased into London's vast Victoria Station, gasping great billows of steam. The Manager's wife gave me a sudden brave smile and a tearful hug. The Manager hastily pressed a few English pounds into my hand "in case of emergency in Dover." I felt a terrible rush of pain. Everything in the station was progressing as if a great play were being acted out on a stage. Carts of flowers, stalls with newspapers and chocolates for sale, porters pushing wagons of luggage, people delicately mounting the train with utter decorum, everyone knowing their part and playing it well except me. I alone seemed confused.

Now the Manager began guiding me to the train steps, wishing me well, telling me to keep my chin up and we'd all hope for the best. "Better days are coming, Rose!" he said, but as the train wheels spun toward the southern coast of England where I would make my crossing to Calais, a great weariness overpowered me. My heart felt like a solid lump in my chest, unconnected by veins and arteries to the rest of my body, unmoving, unable to pump at all. My mind too had stopped. I wasn't thinking. I was no longer even feeling the anguish I had experienced in the London station. My eyes were dry. I thought they too had stopped seeing, even though I was aware of the lovely English countryside that slid past my window mile by mile.

All my dreams were finished. Even my hope of escape was gone. Unreality passed over me. I was a dancer who could no longer dance. I was a sculptor with empty hands. I was married without a husband. I was a Jew with no religion. I was a person without identity or profession or home. When my train braked to a stop in Dover, I was surprised that I was able to stand upright in the aisle. I had thought I might sit forever on the plush seat of the train.

The cold sea air stung my cheeks, and the churning waters of the English Channel stirred up my spirit. I took some deep breaths. I could hear European accents again and languages I understood far better than English! In a few hours I would be in matchless Vienna with my father's family. Vienna would be beautiful. Louis would never find me in that city unfamiliar to him, and I would be among my own. As the ship heaved in the stormy channel waters, I thought I might be able to shake off the despair that held me in its grip.

But Vienna was no longer beautiful. There was a bewildering congestion in the streets, an oppressive strangeness in the air that made ominous the autumn loveliness of the palaces and cathedrals and parks. Jewish people were fleeing the city in alarming numbers, Nazi flags flew from buildings, and all the music that could be heard or played was German. I found myself listening for the Austrian composers that made the city a legend—Mozart, Haydn, Schubert. But they were silenced.

I was deeply shocked by all I was seeing and hearing. There was talk that a German Gestapo officer, Adolf Eichmann, was in Vienna and had set up an office, *Zentralstelle Für Jüdische Auswanderung* (Central Office for Jewish Emigration), and soon this office would be used to force every Jew out of Austria. Jewish leaders who had been arrested were now released by the Nazis to persuade Jews to leave the country. Under Eichmann's orders, even the forbidden *Judische Kulusgemeinde* (Jewish Religious Committee) was reestablished. It was thought that through this organization's forced cooperation with the *Zentralstelle Für Jüdische Auswanderung* all Jews would be expelled. But to where?

It was unbelievable. There were 200,000 Jews in Austria, good Austrian citizens who wouldn't be persuaded that forced emigration would ever become a policy. Although many thousands of Jews eventually did leave Austria (only to be trapped later in other countries), at least a third of Jewish Austrians refused to consider leaving their homeland. My father's relatives were among them. They hung on and hoped that the panic gripping the Jewish people in Austria would subside, and that forced emigration would never take place.

Everyone was in a state of anguished uncertainty—families traveled difficult distances to be together and to try to decide what to do. My own sudden return only added to father's problems. What was he to do with such a large family? There were the very old and the children to consider, and now here was Rose turning up with complete indifference to life or death, and just when they had thought I at least was safe in England!

Some distant relatives of ours from the countryside beyond Vienna had come to the city to confer with our families. They owned an immense estate that had once belonged to a Hungarian count. They were close friends with another Jewish family who owned a carpet factory on adjoining property. This family had two sons, the elder a student in England. They were looking desperately for someone to come and teach them English. I didn't know at the time, but they were planning on emigrating to England and urgently wanted to learn the English language.

It seemed a perfect opportunity to father to get me out of Vienna into the obscurity of the countryside. I would be safe and earn a large salary at the same time. But I wanted to get out of Austria altogether with its swastikas and overflowing streets, the shouting of slogans, and the oppressive Wagnerian music everywhere.

With my usual willfulness, I returned to Piešťany for a mournful reunion. Momma was greatly shocked by how much I had changed, how morose I was, and how indifferent to my future. All our family in Piešťany was also greatly concerned for what the future would hold for Jews in Czechoslovakia. (Piešťany had now been in Czech territory for over twenty years.) Some families were already emigrating, even though the situation was nothing as bad as in Austria. Most Jews hoped to weather the difficulties with fortitude until they were over.

The wealthy carpet manufacturer in Austria knew I had once been very serious about sculpting, that I loved sports and the out-of-doors. In correspondence he pleaded with me to come back to Austria. He offered me a studio in their great house, horses to ride. He promised I would be able to do anything I pleased.

I know if my parents had understood what it was like for Jews in all of Austria, they would never have encouraged me to return there to take the position in the countryside offered to me. Finally to please them, I agreed to go. I was still deeply depressed and convinced that my life was over and that what happened to me didn't matter.

So for a time I went to Austria and taught English. The family made me one of them and treated me as a beloved daughter. It was a pleasant enough life and perhaps the magnificence of the estate, the sports and animals that I loved, the good food, even the sculpting I tried listlessly to do had some healing effect on my emotions, because I began to hope that when this family emigrated to England I would be able to go with them.

Once again negotiations were begun on my behalf. I felt England would be the promised land for me: safe from Hitler, safe from Louis, safe from the chaos falling around me. My parents urged me to go. They felt of all the family I had no one to take care of me, no one to support me in times of troubles. Felice had her Alexander, and my parents had each other. But poor Rose, they reasoned, was alone and had nothing to keep her in Europe anyway. Perhaps from England, I could join my two brothers in America.

I began again to build English castles in the air. But in spite of all efforts a visa to enter England was denied me, and in the end I had to see this dear family go, leaving me grieving with what I felt was again a leftover and shattered life.

Rather than return to Piešťany and enter into the cloud of my family's concern, I decided to go to Budapest, even at the risk of encountering Louis. I had not heard from him for a long time. I still felt I couldn't see him, and I couldn't yet enter into negotiations about a divorce. I just wanted to exist without recognizing that that part of my life had ever happened at all.

I found a room in Budapest and for lack of anything else to do I again entered the Art Academy, doing physiotherapy work part-time to earn money. I didn't dare try to return to Herr Pátzay at his studio. I wasn't even sure he was still there, the past months had brought so many changes to Budapest, and I had no desire left for the struggle to please him.

I had actually fallen out of love with art. The atmosphere at the school had changed dramatically. It seemed students were going through the motions, concentrating on the pretense that the most important issue in existence was the composition of a painting or Matisse's use of color. But we all felt a volcanic trembling, the beginning of a cosmic seizure. The throbbing was in our blood, making even the most disciplined artists restless and disconcerted.

Often I did not bother to go to class but wandered the streets of Budapest, sometimes looking up old friends, often disappointed when I found them. People no longer liked me. No more was I the daredevil Rose, leaping barefoot along the Danube, determined to be famous, making everyone laugh at my antics and admire my brilliant future that seemed so certain.

I began to drift back to the spiritist groups. These devotees were indifferent to living people. They scarcely recognized me or cared that I had gone away and come back again. Such matters concerned them not at all; they only remembered that I had power with the spirits, and for that I was welcome in their midst.

As the weeks passed, I gradually became aware that the spirits I communicated with at the seances did not come at my command and then depart, as I had thought. They remained with me, telling me to do certain things. If I did not obey, they made me very restless. I would pace the floor of my room, full of terrible conflict. Sometimes the spirits would suddenly command me to commit suicide with such force that if I happened to be passing a train, it would take great willpower not to throw myself under its wheels. I began to wonder if the plan to take my life in England had come from these spirits, even though I had then been unaware of them.

Often at seances I conveyed messages from the spirits or communicated with people who were dead. I know now that it was not the dead people who were talking—it was the demons themselves; but at the time I believed that it was the spirits of people who had died. Even high government officials came to my seances to discern the future. Sometimes the spirits gave terrible messages to them, horrors which none of us could then understand.

My sister Felice and Alexander and their little twin boys had left Piešťany and gone to live in Slovakia, in Nitra, a city near the northern border of Czechoslovakia. It was the same city that my mother's parents had come from. Felice's husband had been offered a government job in the Sudeten, a territory of beautiful mountain ranges, so they were happy for this advancement even in such tumultuous times.

But in September of 1938, only a few months after Felice and her husband had moved, the leaders of the opposing world powers, Hitler, Mussolini, England's Chamberlain, and France's Daladier, met for a "peace" conference in Munich. This conference was supposed to avert the worldwide war that was threatening. A peace pact was signed. One of the concessions made to Hitler in an appeasement effort was the agreement that the Sudeten area of Czechoslovakia be immediately occupied by Germany.

For Felice and her husband in Nitra, and all the Jews actually living in Sudetenland, it meant the instant end of their world. Overnight Alexander lost his job, as did almost all the Jews in Sudetenland. Hundreds of Jews wandered the streets, looking for any kind of work, subject to terrible insults and harassment by the Aryan population. Soon food and money were gone. Our family rallied and kept Felice and her family alive.

My oldest brother, Eugene, the doctor, had settled in Moravia. He had married a nurse, the daughter of a wealthy doctor, and they lived in a stately home that had belonged for generations to his wife's family. Eugene, too, gave all the help he could to Felice and Alexander, and for some months was able to see that they did not starve. It was impossible for Felice to get out of Sudetenland, although Eugene tried desperately to bring them to Moravia.

Then in March of 1939 we received terrible news about Eugene. Moravia had been declared a German protectorate, and immediately Nazi storm troops entered Eugene's city. In one day they drove out all the Jews. Eugene and his wife were rushed out of their home, allowed to take only some medical instruments and a few possessions. My dear brother and his genteel wife were raced with others down the streets of his city, ludicrously laden with only the few toppling things they could carry as they ran. They were forced into a poor part of the town, a slum now vacated to become a Jewish ghetto. My brother wrote about what had happened. As he described the terribly overcrowded and unsanitary conditions, he observed humorously that no doctor would become lazy in such a place.

In Budapest I tried to blot out the horror of what was happening. In the seances, I was going into ever deeper trances, letting spirits take possession of my voice and deliver their own messages aloud. Our group began to read the Bible before the

56

seances, in the belief that if we did so, only good spirits would come. The messages from the spirit world were so frightening to us that we began to suppose that they were from evil spirits who wished to abuse or frighten us. It was the good spirits we wanted for communion. The spirits began assuring us that they were of the light and good and that we must not fear them, only obey them and listen to what they had to say.

It was a profoundly strange experience to be conscious, fully able to hear and see, and yet feel oneself to be entirely controlled by other personalities. As our group listened to the spirits, so did I, as if it were not my own lips that were forming the words and my own vocal cords vibrating to make the language come forth. Surely these good spirits would be able to give inner knowledge and guidance in our terrible times.

One day I was invited to a friend's home to meet a man who was himself a medium. People thought because we both had such great "powers" (although I knew by then it was the powers who had me), we ought to be introduced.

No sooner were we introduced than a terrifying thing happened. The demons in him began to quarrel violently with the demons in me. I was utterly unable to understand or control what was happening. His spirits knew everything about me. Often my spirits would tell me to go to the art school and lay my hand on the paper and let them draw. I was afraid to do that, although at home I often wrote whole notebooks full of what they told me to write. Now this man's spirits began cursing my spirits, mocking them that I would not obey them at my art school and calling them names. His spirits began mocking me also, saying that I had a longing for God in my heart, that I wanted to hear about Him. They began to pour forth Scripture verses in scalding scorn. Finally my spirits began shouting that they were bored and had to find amusement in human beings and that I must go to vile places in order to entertain them.

Full of disgust I cried out, "No more! I do not want to be a medium any longer!"

As I said that, horrible punishment began. The spirits lifted me up from the carpet on which I was standing and threw me to the floor. I wrestled desperately to get free from their cursing and beating. I don't know how I escaped out of the room and onto the street and to the home of a friend. Perhaps hours passed in between, but the memory of it is gone.

My friend to whom I fled was also a spiritist. After hearing my story, she immediately called together many of the people who attended my seances. I was terribly shaken and sore, but determined to tell everybody that the spirits that came to us were not good spirits as we had hoped, but evil, lying, unclean spirits. Before I could speak, others began telling of experiencing unusual and frightening things: obscene messages from what they had thought to be "departed spirits of loved ones," pictures crashing down from the walls of rooms, stranglings, cursings. We were all greatly unsettled and wondered what to do. We had started many of our seances with the reading of the Bible, and someone in the group hit upon the idea of consulting the Bible to see if in its pages there might be a formula for dealing with matters of this nature. It was the great mercy of God that we finally came upon the passage in Isaiah 8: "And when they say to you, 'Consult the mediums and the wizards who whisper and mutter,' should not a people consult their God? Should they consult the dead on behalf of the living?"

It wasn't that any of us really believed the Bible as the Word of God, but we respected it as a holy book with spiritual insights. These words struck us with force and authority. As we continued to search the Bible we found the verse in Leviticus 20:27: "As for a man or a woman, if there is a medium or a spiritist among them, they shall surely be put to death; they shall be stoned with stones, their bloodguiltiness is upon them."

I began to shake with fright. I knew I was in the grip of the demons that had fought within me. Now added to it was the doom predicted for me in our Jewish Scriptures. I began to weep, declaring I wanted no more to do with the demons. I wanted to be free of them. I wanted them to go away.

Suddenly the demons in me began to cry out horribly. I was as terrified as the others. Then the spirits lifted me up and again threw me to the floor. They began beating me. I struggled to ward off the invisible blows, but I could only scream for mercy. My friends tried to hold me but were driven off by the demons, who continued to pull at me from different directions. I thought they would tear me in two. The harder I thrashed and tried to free myself, the harder the spirits dug into my flesh.

The group of people in the room became hysterical. No one knew what to do. My friend was a nominal Protestant. In desperation she began to recite the Lord's Prayer. I had never heard it before, but I shouted it after her, word by word, over and over, perspiration pouring down my face, my voice hoarse with pain. Gradually the hold of the spirits seemed to weaken. Their wailing became less vicious and more piteous, and finally they were quiet.

But I knew they had not really left me. As the days passed, I was in constant distress from the demons. I had to pretend for the sake of my physiotherapy patients that nothing was wrong with me. Everyone in Budapest was nervous and restless at the end of 1938, especially the Jewish people, so no one was surprised that I seemed under intense stress.

News came that Eugene was transported from the ghetto to a concentration camp in Czechoslovakia. My Aunt Hermine and her husband and other aunts were taken to the same camp. I knew nothing then about concentration camps, other than that they were dreadful places, and I in Budapest and my family in Piešťany lived day by day in the desperate hope that somehow Eugene would be released. In the camp Eugene was allowed to work as a doctor, and we were permitted at first to send him food parcels and letters. We lived on any comfort we could invent: if there was a war, he would be needed. He would be released. Because he had to treat hundreds of people, he needed strength; he would receive enough to eat and would receive better treatment than other prisoners. How foolish all these hopes seem now.

Then came the news that a young cousin from Vienna had been sent with hundreds of others to Dachau! This was the first concentration camp to be set up in Germany itself and had already existed for five years. The commandant at Dachau was rumored to be a man who had once been a patient in a psychiatric clinic, and the stories that had filtered out to East Europe about this camp were unspeakable. My relatives were frantic. They raised an enormous sum of money to give to the Nazis for the ransom of my cousin. After some months he was allowed to get out, but he was so terrified of the Nazis he wouldn't tell a word of what he had been through.

In Czechoslovakia mother wrote that all Jews were ordered to wear the yellow armband with the Star of David on their sleeves. Jewish shops were closed, or simply given to non-Jews. Professional men such as judges and university professors were sweeping the streets and collecting garbage. Any citizen could freely attack a Jew and beat him. Bands of Nazi youths roamed the streets, smashing windows, looting, throwing children into the road. Signs began to appear with hate slogans.

By this time my father was an old man and out of work. He was immensely agitated by the atrocities, and beside himself with worry about Eugene in the concentration camp and Felice hungry in Nitra. The indignations were great. Old men like Poppa who had cared for large families all their lives suddenly found themselves helpless to protect their loved ones from brutal, random outrages. It was too much for my father. One day, agitated beyond his strength, he had a heart attack and died.

By this time, travel between Hungary and Czechoslovakia was prohibited. Even the news about Poppa was greatly delayed. When word came to me, he was already buried. I sat in my room in Budapest, stunned at Poppa's death. At that time I had been studying some prints I had of Michelangelo's Sistine Ceiling in the Vatican Chapel. The beautiful pictures of God he painted perplexed me deeply. Michelangelo depicted God as a *man*. This was inconceivable to my Jewish mind. I simply could not grasp what this great genius was trying to communicate about God.

The death of my father drove me to think about Michelangelo's God, not in my intellectual Gnostic way, nor as a spiritist. A raw unrelenting grief ached and throbbed in every bone in my body. There was no one to help me, no one to give me any consolation. In my desperation I began to read the Bible we had used at the spiritist meetings.

I knew Jewish people read the Bible and I recalled the book of Job. In the synagogue I had attended as a tiny child, I remembered that the men sat on the floor reading from Job and from the Psalms. I too got onto the floor of my room and tried to sit as I remembered the men had sat. I didn't know the traditions, or prayers that should be said. I began reading the book of Job. To my great disappointment I couldn't understand it.

I thought if I studied it I would be able to comprehend its

meaning. Over and over I repeated the entire book, but it was unintelligible to me. My desperation increased. I felt the Bible *had* to help me.

I turned to the Psalms. Psalms are read every day of the year by Jews, and in times of sorrow we turn even more to this book of David. I started reading psalms, but they too made no sense. My tears poured onto the pages, but they contained only strings of words without meaning.

For a week I stayed in my room, mourning my father, and reading book after book of the Bible in a hopeless, desperate way. The Jewish calendar was drawing near to the Day of Atonement, the holiest of days for Jews. A great sense of sin fell upon me. I was already through the whole Bible and reading the last chapter of the book of Revelation. I was greatly distressed. I read that outside the heavenly City were those who have strayed from God, and sorcerers and the immoral and murderers and idolaters and all who love to lie. My face flamed with conviction. I felt the words were an exact description of my own self. Even the reference to murderers described me because if I had been home with my father, I was sure I could have eased his distress and perhaps saved his life. When he was in his greatest need I had been in Budapest, attending concerts and seances, wasting my life with no thought for anyone but myself.

Yet the words "Come, come, come" of the book of Revelation tormented me. On the evening of the beginning of the Day of Atonement, I began to fast. It was the only thing I knew to do.

In Budapest I had a friend, also called Rose. In many ways she was a bizarre person. She was a vegetarian, and she used to go to vegetarian restaurants that were run by Gentile Seventh-Day Adventist groups. I remember we once went to one of their meetings. The first thing the Adventists told me was that I would have to give up art and sculpting to please God. Rose and I laughed and left.

But Rose read the New Testament. I dragged my exhausted body to her apartment. Perhaps Rose would read the Bible with me and be able to explain it. She was the only person in the world I knew who actually read the Bible because she wanted to.

Rose answered her door with a look of astonishment. I knew there were black shadows under my eyes. I felt unsteady on my feet. Quickly she sat me down and made me some tea. As I drank, she told me about some meetings she had been attending where the Bible was very clearly explained. The meetings were held on Sunday nights. I wanted Rose to explain the meaning of the Bible, but she insisted that she could not. If I would go to these meetings, I could learn.

I was in a fever of anticipation for Sunday evening to come. When it finally arrived and I found the building in Budapest where the meeting was being held, I very nearly didn't get in. In my haste I had come to a locked entrance. I rushed around the building several times before someone directed me to what was called "The Gospel Hall." It was a large room on the second floor of the building. That Sunday night was September 24, 1939.

IV

The New Beginning

BEFORE I CAME INTO THE ROOM I could hear singing. It washed over me like a hot wave and wrenched my heart. I loved music and I loved to hear hymns. I was instantly reminded of the little YWCA meetings in England. It wasn't until a few moments had passed that I realized that I was actually hearing English sung. That intrigued me so I was even more eager to enter the meeting, even though the room was already completely full.

An usher led me to an empty place in the first row. I joined in the singing, my eyes stinging with tears. I was suddenly exhausted and very depressed.

After several hymns, people settled back into their chairs and an American missionary began to speak. At that time I didn't know what a missionary was, but I had attended so many strange meetings that I was accustomed not to know exactly how things fit together. A missionary and a medium didn't seem so far apart to me then!

The speaker began to talk about the Messiah. I was astonished. I had assumed that the meeting was for Christians. That the talk would be about Jewish matters was an amazing thing to me. The message was called, "Behold the Man." The missionary spoke from the Old Testament, showing how the Jewish prophecies were fulfilled in the New Testament in Jesus. I was fascinated. Time after time, beginning with the prophecy of Jesus' birth and going all the way through to His rejection and death, the missionary showed that Jesus Christ was the Jewish Messiah.

After the hymns and prayers that concluded the meeting, I stepped up to the speaker, a Mr. Miller. (There had been no invitation to receive Christ as Savior because that was not the custom in Hungary.)

"I am a Jewess," I began, "but I believe in Jesus." The man looked at me strangely. For one thing, I was dressed completely in black because of my father's death. And I spoke in such a defensive manner that my words had a hollow ring.

Mr. Miller began to ask me about God. I had been reading the Bible constantly since my father's death—not understanding a word, but even a parrot can speak. I remember quoting the first verse of the Gospel of John to him.

Quietly he asked me about the devil. I simply smiled at him. I didn't believe he was serious. Even after all I had experienced with the spiritists, even after the nightmare experience when spirits had tried to pull me apart, I was still so blinded, I felt a little like laughing. When I saw that he was waiting for an answer, I replied that the devil was just an evil thought. "No!" He responded so vehemently I was taken aback. He invited me to sit down. Then he began to tell me that man was created perfect. On my face I have a tiny dark freckle. You can hardly see it. But the missionary said, "You see, you have this tiny little spot. Even you are not perfect. Because Adam and Eve fell into sin, now all human beings are sinful because of Adam. It was the devil, in the form of a serpent, who came to Eve to tempt her and lead mankind into sin. Now we are all spoiled by sin."

"Where is all this written?" I challenged him. I was very surprised when he replied, "In the Bible."

I gathered up my purse and Bible to leave. Before I could get away, he told me that he and his wife could be reached at a nearby bookstore. We made an appointment to meet again.

As soon as I got home, I opened my Bible and began to look for the places where it wrote about the devil. It was very late at night, but I didn't notice the time. Page after page I turned, looking with absolutely no success for references to the devil. I desperately wanted to prove Mr. Miller wrong or to find out for myself if the improbable things he was teaching were true. Finally I went to bed exhausted.

As soon as morning came, I hurried to the bookstore. I was so eager to tell this man that he was wrong! I had found no mention of the devil. Perhaps Mr. Miller was surprised to see me appear like a strange black crow with piercing tired eyes. Perhaps he was not. Already he was praying for me.

Without any preliminaries, when I saw him I burst out, "Well, I couldn't find the devil in the Bible."

Pulling up a chair again, he smiled at me as if it were the most natural thing in the world to be discussing such things even before half of Budapest was awakened to another anxious day.

"Well, he's in there!" he smiled. And then he began to tell me the gospel from the very beginning. This time I insisted he show me every verse to prove what he was saying. I put pieces of paper in the Bible to mark the pages on which were verses we discussed. I knew I could never find them again, and I wanted the chance to look at them later for myself. After a while my Bible had a forest of white strips of paper growing out of the top. Mr. Miller showed me that I was lost—a sinner in need of a Redeemer. He talked too about the fearful times in which we lived and the need to have one's life right before God.

Days before, I had gone into a shop in Budapest to buy some bread, and a woman looked at me with hatred and said in a terrible voice, "Jewess!" The experience merely humiliated me. I was not afraid. I was desperately worried about Eugene in the camp, and my sister and her family having to live in terror in their Nazi city. But even with all that, the possibility of my own danger in Hungary seemed remote. The urgency of Mr. Miller's warning didn't penetrate my heart. The idea of being a sinner was too new to make an impression on me. I wasn't even completely sure I believed in God the way the missionary talked about Him.

We agreed to meet again the next day. Again I went back to my apartment to read the Bible, turning the pages carefully so as not to lose any of the paper strips that marked the pages.

That night as I read, a strange thing began to happen. There was an inner change as I studied the Scriptures. I was no longer a skeptic, looking for "proofs" so that I could dispute Mr. Miller's odd ideas. I wasn't thinking that I knew better than he. I just wanted to learn. I didn't know that even then at the Gospel Hall, many people were praying earnestly for the young Jewess in black who talked for hours about the Bible.

I read great portions of the Bible, moving from the Old Testament to the New Testament and back again, aware more and more of an agitation that impelled me to discover the truth. Over and over I read Isaiah 53 and Psalm 22. My heart was deeply touched.

The next day Mr. Miller asked me if I could believe in the virgin birth. I felt this was no problem because I reasoned that if God could create Adam and Eve, since they were not born as other human beings are born, then Messiah Himself could certainly come in a miraculous way. We went on to the subject of hell. I had studied countless hideous paintings of hell and thought them grotesque depictions of the black forces within humankind. Since I hadn't actually believed in God, the idea of hell as real didn't occur to me. I had no fear of eternal punishment. But by Tuesday morning, I was able to learn about hell.

When Mr. Miller talked about Poppa being in hell, I became very upset and couldn't think of such a thing. Even today, as much as I believe that we have to be born again, I have to say that my father had never heard the gospel. I just leave it to God. He is a righteous judge and I leave it in His hands. But that morning it hurt me terribly to imagine Poppa in such a dreadful place. Mr. Miller gently pleaded with me not to go there. Even as I was putting pieces of paper in my Bible I was thinking, "I will never go to that place." I told Mr. Miller I had to go home and read again the verses we had discussed.

I was now thirty years old. All my life I had lived in a condition of spiritual confusion. As a child I had suffered much because of my stubbornness, a rebellion I myself couldn't understand. In my student days as a dancer and artist and sculptor, I had fed on any ideas that came along, no matter how fearful or destructive. The mockery of my marriage, the ruin of every plan or dream I had, the thwarted idea of suicide, the despair of my father's death, the horror of the times, all pressed upon me. For the first time in my life, I had found a gleam of light that grew brighter and brighter the closer I drew to it.

I was reading the third chapter of the Gospel of John, where Jesus tells Nicodemus he must be born again. Born again! If only that were possible! Not to be Rose but to start my life again. But always I spoiled everything. Others too had humiliated me, disappointed me, led me into cesspools of destruction. Foul spirits had used my body, had almost torn me apart. The light was too bright! I felt I could not bear the distress that over-whelmed me.

But at the same time I became conscious of the mercy of God, deeper than the deepest sea. A God who didn't allow me to be killed in all my daredevil antics of youth, who kept me from suicide when so many times I felt impelled toward it. His unseen hand had even protected me from the fury of Satan when he tried to suffocate and kill me. Over and over when I had been at the brink of destruction God had always overruled the circumstances and rescued me, even without my knowing it was Him, even when I was such a sinner I mocked Him and disbelieved in Him!

I don't remember getting to my knees in that little room. But I remember praying, all my terrible pride utterly gone. It had been three days since I had first heard the Bible preached and the gospel gradually explained to me. But I knew what to do. With everything in me I gave my heart to the Messiah, to the Savior, to the Lord Jesus Christ. At the very same moment I also gave my life to Him. I knew how worthless it was to me. Born again! A new life! Not Rose anymore!

I had to laugh. Perhaps it wasn't reverent, but I laughed with joy and relief! All my life I had been looking for something better and higher than what I knew. And all the time it was Jesus I had sought. There was no one with me, no one to enjoy the joke, to laugh with me! I seized my Bible and began reading again in Isaiah. Every word seemed written for me. I understood perfectly! I came to the verse in Isaiah 38:17: "Lo, for my own welfare I had great bitterness; It is Thou who hast kept my soul from the pit of nothingness, for Thou hast cast all my sins behind Thy back." A great lightness came over me. I felt my spirit leaping and dancing as so long ago I had danced with my body. I turned back to Isaiah 32:17: "And the work of righteousness will be peace, and the service of righteousness, quietness and confidence forever."

Peace! I was flooded with it! I was amazed. I felt I must look different. My face in the mirror gazed back rapturously at me. After all the years of anxiety and striving and longing! To have found peace! It was very late. I think I would have run out into the street and told people what had happened to me if it hadn't been for the hour. I went to bed not aware of any tiredness, and fell asleep instantly.

The next morning I went quickly to the Gospel Hall. I was so excited I hardly knew how to speak. I didn't need words. By just looking at my face they knew what had happened! They were all very happy, naturally, but they didn't tell me that. They listened peacefully to my extravagant enthusiasm. I remember telling them they would have to put more chairs in the Hall right away because I was going straight out to tell people that it was Jesus the Messiah for whom they were looking. Nobody had told me for so long.

I was indignant. "Think how much suffering I could have been spared if I had only known!" I declared. "If someone would have opened his mouth to tell me about the love of God, how the Lord Jesus left the glories of heaven and took upon Himself a human form and came down to be my Redeemer, my Savior, my Messiah, willing to forgive me and take all my sins upon Himself on the cross and in exchange give me His righteousness, His peace . . ."

Mr. Miller smiled warmly as he gently suggested that there was even more to learn. A very great deal of Bible teaching that I would want to know. Of course I wanted to learn everything. I was eager if there was more to know. But surely somebody could at least give me some tracts and I would go out and hand them around to people on the streets. There were hundreds of people walking about with grieving, desperate hearts. Everyone was afraid of what the war would mean. Germany had already occupied Poland. Even though the Nazis would never attack neutral Hungary, people were fearful. I didn't want anyone to suffer one day longer!

"To think how far I have traveled! To Austria! To England! All over Hungary and Czechoslovakia! And no one in all these places in all that time told me about Jesus! Why in Hungary"—I grasped the arm of the startled missionary's wife, "in Hungary, half the population is Protestant! And no one ever told me about Jesus!"

Mr. and Mrs. Miller had themselves begun the Gospel Hall in Budapest. With the coming of war, they knew it was uncertain how long they would be able to stay. They were eager for me to learn all I could. There was a small evangelical seminary in Budapest that they were associated with and they took me there. I was a faithful visitor, studying the Bible constantly. I realized how very little I knew after all, in spite of my salvation. The missionaries and teachers gave me hours and hours of instruction, as if I were the only person in the world with whom they were concerned.

Because of the war, it was forbidden to hand out printed material on the street corners or in the parks, but I distributed Christian tracts anyway. I gave up everything I had been doing with my time—the art lessons, the concerts, studying at the galleries and museums. Studying the Bible at the seminary and talking to people about the Lord Jesus filled every spare minute of every day.

I still had to work to support myself, and I continued working with some physiotherapy patients. As I worked, I talked constantly to the patients about God and salvation and about the peace I had found. Some liked it, but most soon got tired of me. Most of them thought I was a bit crazy, and certainly a fanatic.

They made me remember what Felice used to say to me! "Ah, Rose, *you* will never be crazy!" She meant by that that I was crazy already.

I expected Felice to be even more convinced of my craziness when I wrote her that I had received Jesus as my personal Savior and as my Jewish Messiah. At this time it was very difficult to travel from Budapest to Slovakia because of political tension. So I wrote to all my relatives about Jesus. I tried to communicate with all my old friends, either to go to them or to write them, but often it was very difficult. Everyone was moving about Europe, trying to get away from the war, to get to the war, to return to their homes, to find their families. Jews especially turned up or disappeared without notice, so it was very hard.

One old friend I was able to find was a woman called Vera. She came from a part of Hungary that is now Romania. Vera's father had been a poor country rabbi, but Vera and her sister Sarah were Communists. I was anxious that Vera and Sarah and Sarah's young husband become believers; and after much prayer and work with them, they received Jesus as Messiah. It was wonderful! Through them I came to know many "Christian Orthodox Jews," and I discovered I needed to learn even more in order to witness to these people, who were nominal Christians without salvation.

Mr. Miller was gifted in personal evangelism. In watching him, I learned how to give without sparing myself and how to be true to the Bible. I saw that everything depended on the fact that the Bible is God's Word—that it is true. If the Bible says something, that is the final word on the subject. The hunger I had for the Bible grew the more I learned.

Two weeks after I became a believer, I told Mr. and Mrs. Miller that I wanted to leave everything behind and become a missionary too. They were pleased, but with reservations. "She has a strong fire in her heart now, but she has had so many professions already, she wants to try out a new one."

Thankfully they decided to give me a test.

"Do you know what the hardest mission field is?" they asked. "It is being a missionary to the Jews! The very work you are proposing to give your life to!"

I did not become a saint overnight. But their words made me swell with determination. "I don't care!" I responded. "This is the only thing I can do and the only thing I want to do! I want to be a witness. I can't speak of anything else, I can't think of anything else, I can't read anything else except the Bible. I can't continue with my regular work, anyway. My patients can't stand it when I talk to them all the time about the Lord Jesus, and I can't stand not to!"

The autumn of 1939 was hardly the best of times to begin a missionary life. Winter was soon approaching, and it was getting very cold out-of-doors. Indoors there was no fuel. Food was scarce. German soldiers marched through Hungary, and our own supplies were taken to the battlefield to be used against Poland. Later even what was left to us would be confiscated and used in the massive Nazi attack against Russia.

Mr. and Mrs. Miller warned me that I would suffer. People didn't have food. Certainly there would be no money to give to a new missionary. Our government made it illegal to hold meetings and distribute literature. Everything was in turmoil. But I was resolute. I had once abandoned all my life to art. I had said I would die for art. How much more willing was I to give my life to Jesus and if necessary to die for him!

I am forever thankful for the training the Millers gave me. They taught me the importance of memorizing Scripture, of having a prayer life, of keeping a prayer list. Our studying of the Scriptures went on. A day never passed without Bible study. Often I spent time going out in the streets witnessing. Sometimes I stayed at the seminary to help Mr. Miller in his work of translating materials from English into Hungarian.

As I was preparing for missionary service, my patients that still remained defended themselves against my gospel onslaught by asking questions that I couldn't answer. Often I returned to the Gospel Hall or the seminary weeping because of my ignorance. Mr. Miller stressed that I must depend on the Word of God and not the wisdom of men.

Once I was to visit some friends who were Jews, but attended a Protestant church. One of them was a lawyer, and I was terrified that he would ask me questions that I could not answer. I asked Mr. Miller if I could please phone him for answers if I got into trouble in the discussion. He shook his head vigorously. "No. Do not phone me, Rose! Phone up!" He meant, "Call upon God!" It was advice that has lasted me all my life.

We held public Bible studies in a large flat loaned to us by a believer. I was able to invite many people there. Mr. Miller would give greetings to the group in his broken Hungarian or Czechoslovakian, and then he would begin to teach in English.

I translated for him, concentrating not only on the words he said, but also on the scriptural meaning. Because I had to repeat everything he said, it was an opportunity for me to learn how to present the gospel and how to teach from the Bible. The Lord knew how to quickly give me the education I needed.

In the tumult of Budapest in 1939, our minds were filled with the urgency to preach the gospel and win as many souls to Christ as we could. Everything was uncertain. Hitler's storm troops swept country by country invincibly across Europe.

Poland, invaded September 1, 1939, was overrun in four

weeks. By April of 1940, the Nazis occupied Denmark and Norway, after a bombardment that lasted only two months. In May 1940, Belgium and Holland were invaded, opening the period of Hitler's *blitzkrieg* (lightning war). By using tanks by land and planes by air, the Netherlands fell in four days, Belgium in four weeks, and France within seven weeks. All Europe was in a state of shock.

During this early time of the war, I tried desperately to get a permit to leave Budapest to visit my family in Slovakia. Finally the visa came through. Mrs. Miller loaned me a big suitcase packed with tracts and Bibles so I could make the trip an evangelistic journey, and I set out by train to be reunited with my parents and relatives, still together in Slovakia.

In spite of the train packed with soldiers and the wartime tension and anxieties, it was a wonderful journey to my home. Never had Hungary seemed so beautiful: the lovely rounded hills, the church steeples in the distance, the vineyards stretching endlessly to the horizon. Every sight enchanted me: a small lake glittering in a field, the purple sweep of the sky, the yellow and white towns through which we passed, some over a thousand years old, the great oak forests.

Finally the train braked at the border between Hungary and Slovakia for customs inspection. Our crossing was at a small village, and I thought I would have no trouble. But to be carrying so much literature in wartime and across a border! The guards were furious. It didn't matter that I tried to explain it was Bible literature. I pled in Hungarian, I pled in Slovakian, and then in Czech. Even knowing several languages made me suspect. My suitcase was confiscated, but I was permitted to continue. I was greatly disappointed not to have the suitcase. I wanted gospel literature to give Momma and Felice and all my other relations!

It was an immense relief to arrive at Felice's doorstep. It happened that she was ill when I arrived, bedridden with phlebitis and not allowed to stand up. Because of Felice's illness, my mother came to see us in her home and I was able to tell Momma and Felice and her husband and their two little boys about the great mercy of the Lord.

For hours I sat by Felice's bedside, my mother in another chair in the room, and read the Gospels to them. Mother said very little, although what I taught was hard for a Jew to accept. In those terrifying war years, numbers of Jewish people were entering Protestant and Catholic churches. It wasn't that they believed, but they thought if they were members of a Christian church the persecution against them would stop. With some, perhaps, it helped for a little while. In the end it meant nothing. It was not Jewish souls the Nazis sought. It was Jewish blood.

Such pragmatic action would have been unthinkable for my mother. Mother wouldn't even hear of going into hiding, as some did, for a while. She said, "At seventy-three what does anyone want with me?" How little any of us knew at that time.

Mother listened to the gospel and Felice listened, and whatever they thought, both of them marveled at the change that had come over me. It had been years since they had seen me happy. The gripping depression, the lassitude, the earlier driving ambition and restlessness were gone. Sometimes when I laughed or sang little hymns as I worked, Momma would faintly smile in return. Even if she didn't understand and couldn't accept my new life, she was glad all the same to see me happy.

When Felice was well again, the two of us returned to the border customs office to see if I could get my suitcase returned. My visa was almost expired, but I so desperately wanted to leave some literature with my family that I prayed earnestly that somehow God would help me get back the materials.

I was overjoyed to discover that the valise had not been sent "to headquarters for examination" as the guards had declared. It remained in that tiny village depot office. At first the guards absolutely refused to return it. They insisted they were not competent to examine the literature and make a decision. But the more they said "No," the more I persisted, taking out tracts and reading word for word to the guards until they squirmed with boredom and discomfort.

Every time one of them made a motion to close the suitcase, I pulled something else from it and showed them in great detail that it was a Bible or New Testament. I read passages from different sections, insisting that I was a missionary and that everything in the suitcase was nothing more than God's Word. I suppose they couldn't help but believe I was a missionary. I was quite happy to stay all day preaching to them, and in the end they gave in and sent Felice and me off with my suitcase. I was thrilled to have the literature back, even though in the very few days I had left with my family I knew there would be no time to distribute it.

Felice had listened patiently to my "preaching" to the guards. When we returned to her home, she took some of the Christian material I gave her and promised to read it.

I had been with many other members of my family during that visit. They were amazed at my joyful spirit, considering the tension of the times. They listened with bewilderment at what I had to say about Jesus, the Messiah, but they were not angry. We did a lot of talking about Momma, too. At her age, if it became necessary, she would be unable to hide or flee, and it was decided that she should try to get to America to live with my two brothers there. Mother was pleased at the thought of seeing her two sons again, and I think she realized what a worry she was to everyone. She agreed to try to escape and even began learning English.

It was tremendously expensive and difficult to get a passport and visa to leave Slovakia, even when one had relatives in America as sponsors. Anti-Semitism was rampant, and it was very dangerous for a Jew to travel to a major city to the American Embassy for the necessary permissions. A great deal of work and "arranging" had to be done, but sometime after I returned to Budapest I received word that Momma would be traveling by guarded bus to the Embassy in Budapest with some other people who were trying to get out.

When Momma's bus arrived in Budapest, the Jews were allowed out only into the American Embassy. They were not permitted to technically "enter" the city itself, so I and a few other relatives went to see Momma at the Embassy. I was allowed to bring in food from a nearby restaurant, and it was so important an occasion that I invited Mr. and Mrs. Miller to come with me to meet my mother.

Momma was so excited and happy, she even kissed Mr. Miller and thanked him for helping her Rose find peace. We ate and drank hot tea that the Americans gave us. After awhile Mr. and Mrs. Miller left. But things did not go as we had thought. It was true that Momma had the permission of the American government to go to America, but there was a problem. There was no country through which she needed to pass that was willing to give entrance to Jews. Hours of negotiations ensued. There was one way, an Embassy official suggested doubtfully, eyeing Mother's obvious frailty. She could possibly arrange to travel across Russia and leave for America through some port in the Far East.

But alone? And at her age? Momma was aghast. Even I would have faltered at such an ordeal, and I was still young and athletic and in the prime of my strength. Finally Momma collected her belongings, and pretending it was not so important, walked out of the Embassy and onto the bus to return to Felice. I watched her with aching eyes. It was the last time I ever saw her.

In Hungary in those early war years, it was a time of tremendous upheaval and confusion. Because of our central geography, there were more crossings of troops, political upheavals, and redrawings of the map than in earlier periods of our history ten times as long.

Once Hungary and Austria were together in the great Austro-Hungarian Empire I knew as a tiny child. Even after independence, Hungary always had close ties with Austria. In 1938 in April, Hitler succeeded in accomplishing the *Anschluss*, the union of Germany and our beloved Austria. This was a terrible shock to the whole of Hungary, and there were divisions inside Hungary as to where loyalties ought to be placed and in what direction our future lay.

Already in Germany madness ruled. In Hitler, Germany had a leader who was to set up a new world order. A fatalistic belief in the inevitability of the supreme victory of the Third Reich gripped Hungary as well as elated Germany. The bulk of our people were convinced that Hitler was invincible and that Hungary's survival was only possible by supporting the Nazis. Into Hungary came the terrible anti-Jewish laws. This is why Momma had so much trouble traveling to Budapest on public transport and had to hire a guarded bus.

Hitler rewarded our country for its support by granting Hungary a choice territory that had been taken over by Czechoslovakia. By this means, he turned our neutral premier, Bela Imredy, into a fervent Nazi. Premier Imredy had been a devout Roman Catholic and a man in whom the anti-Nazi groups in Hungary, including us Jews, had placed high hopes. But so avid a Nazi did Imredy become that he had made a speech on Christmas Eve of 1938 declaring that "one drop of Jewish blood was enough to infect a man's patriotism and character." It was tragically ironic because no sooner had he said this than he was discovered to have had a Jewish great-grandmother. Our ruling Regent publicly showed him the document that proved his ancestry, and Imredy fainted. The Regent took the opportunity to appoint another premier in his place (one not so sympathetic to the Nazis), and Imredy, after a period of recovery, turned out in the end to be the leader of a Nazi opposition party.

Our new premier, Count Teleki, was determined to keep Hungary independent, but at the same time he hoped to squeeze out of German "friendship" anything he could that would benefit Hungary. At first it worked. Hitler awarded more territory to Hungary, and again our borders were shifted outward. There were mass returns and departures of peoples, and the personal confusion and sufferings of our people were immense.

The population upheavals reached even to Budapest. I knew many languages and when I was not studying the Bible and translating for the Millers, I was on the streets, passing out literature and talking to the milling crowds of refugees.

Our mission translation work continued feverishly. The Millers knew the time was very short for Americans to be able to stay in Europe. Many evenings we worked preparing literature far into the night, often taking a break at eleven o'clock to listen to the news and drink tea.

In 1941, all Hungary was shocked to learn that our premier, Count Teleki, had shot himself. The Regent was forced to appoint a Nazi as premier, and life in Hungary grew suddenly very bad for Jews. In August of 1941, the government rounded up some 17,000 stateless Jews who had sought refuge in Hungary, and pushed them into the Ukraine. The Germans were already occupying this territory and seized thousands of these Jews for slave labor. The rest vanished. It was horrifying.

I was translating during the many meetings we had in those times. Night after night, Mr. Miller pled with the people, many of them Jews, who crowded into our mission hall, "Come unto Me, all ye that labor and are heavy laden, and I will give you rest." Many people were won to the Lord in the last days of his ministry in Budapest.

One night, very late, I returned to the tiny room I rented near the hall to find a small postcard from Felice waiting for me. She mailed postcards because the censors let them go through more quickly than letters. I sat on my bed in the dim light of my room and pulled off my shoes as I read the card. Her words were characteristically forthright, but poetry or music couldn't have transported me more.

"Rose, I have accepted the Lord Jesus as my Messiah. I knew you would want to know. I am praying for Alexander."

I have accepted Jesus as Messiah! I was suddenly in a delirium of happiness. I longed to be with her, to embrace her and laugh and cry and pray and join with her in prayer for her husband and children and our mother. All my tiredness and anxiety melted away, and I lay on my bed praising God and pleading anew with Him for the rest of our family.

It had been only two months after my visit that Felice gave her heart to the Lord Jesus. She had been reading the Bible and the literature I gave her. It was not easy in the beginning because Felice, like Momma, always stuck to her Jewishness. And to pray to Jesus! To her, that seemed like turning to another God! But God spoke through the Scriptures and Felice responded. She was able to pray to Jesus as her Savior and Lord. And very soon after, she started to distribute those same tracts that I had left in her home because I had too much to carry! While she was distributing tracts on the street, she met a Christian who took her to a Gospel hall in her town. And so the Lord led her to those with whom she could fellowship. Even Momma went with her sometimes to the meetings.

In Felice's town things were very bad. Her husband, because he had special skills, was needed and had a work permit. But hundreds of Jews had gone into hiding. For most there was no work. Thousands had been packed on transports for forced-labor conscription. Felice was able to get food for Momma because of her husband's job. Most Jews existed on starvation rations.

By this time it was the summer of 1941. We were still having openair meetings in Budapest and giving the gospel to Gentiles and Jews alike. One day Mr. and Mrs. Miller disappeared. Karl, an American worker at the mission, came running to me to tell me the Millers were in prison. We were horrified! How could it happen? They were Americans! But even their American citizenship could not save them from the fact that they were also Jews!

The first thing I did was organize an all-day and all-night prayer meeting for them. Some of the Christians were on vacation in the country, but anyone I could find I brought together so that prayer would not stop for the Millers. Then Karl left for the office of the American Consulate. It was several days before he could get an appointment. The Consulate was in pandemonium: so many people demanding attention, so much pleading and urgency and tears and terror.

Finally Karl managed to get permission to visit the Millers in prison. We went together. The women were locked on one side of the prison, the men on the other. The Millers were imprisoned with murderers and raving people and every kind of criminal. In spite of their ordeal, they were patient and quiet. Mr. Miller said it would be only a matter of time before they were released by the Consulate and that God never makes mistakes. It was heartrending to see them in such degrading circumstances, and tears poured down my face as we walked home from the prison. People no longer paid attention to people weeping on the streets.

Mr. Miller was my spiritual father, and he had become a real father to me. How patiently he had taught me! Not only had I learned how to read and memorize the Bible, but he had drilled simple principles of Bible study into me. "What is the main point of this passage? To whom is the Word of God speaking in these verses? What does this mean in everyday life?"

One of the best things he taught me was to memorize the chapter and verse of any Scripture. Because I could speak several languages, he was concerned that I would become confused if I did not. He would say playfully, "If you go to a city, you have to know the name of the city. You have to know the name of the street and also the number."

My heart twisted in grief at the thought of such good and loving people locked up in that overflowing prison, separated from each other and subjected to all kinds of abuses. We at the mission kept a prayer vigil for them. It was an overwhelming comfort and relief to put our concern and love before God and to entrust them utterly into the hands of our loving Father in heaven.

After several long days, the American Consulate secured the Millers' release. Along with their freedom came the instruction that they must leave Europe immediately. But in the prison Mr. Miller's eyes had been opened. He made time during the hectic days of packing to sit down with me and ask me what I was going to do. He told me I was in the greatest danger. Actually I was torn in two directions.

With all my being, I knew God had called me to be a witness for Jesus Christ to my own Jewish people. I knew they distrusted Gentiles and that worshiping Jesus seemed like idolatry to them. I understood their hearts because my own heart was Jewish. My Jewishness enlarged even as my love for Jesus grew.

There was a young American missionary called Mary working alone high in the hills along the Polish border, in an area inside the Soviet Union. She was beautiful, both in body and in spirit, and anyone who met her was immediately struck by her sweetness and spiritual authority. She had a large orphanage in the mountains where she gathered to her all the forlorn, traumatized children who were war victims. Some had lost their parents in bombings. Some had been separated in the mass movements of people. Some parents had already gone to the camps. There were always children in those poverty-stricken areas who for one reason or another were unwanted and left in the woods.

Mary had met me in Budapest, where she came for supplies. She urged me to come to her orphanage and help her. Her area was densely populated by Jewish people in scores of tiny villages —hundreds of the poorest of people she had no way of reaching with the gospel, and their needs were great. Perhaps work at the orphanage would not take up all my time, and I could travel to those people. It was hard for anybody to say no to Mary, and I wavered. But Mr. Miller had been adamant.

"Rose," he declared vehemently, "if you have started to be a missionary to the Jewish people, then you stay with it. You will have many good offers, but stick to it. If you want the blessing of the Lord, do not leave your first love. It is to the Jews you are to witness. This is your work."

Deep within myself, I knew Mr. Miller was right.

I had declined Mary's offer with real reluctance. She had smiled with her luminous eyes and told me she would be praying about it. Now I was wondering again if I ought not to go and help Mary in the mountains. Life for people even in Budapest was increasingly precarious. In the barren, crowded little villages where Mary was trying to minister, existence would be desperate.

But the Lord kept me on course. I began receiving invitations from Baptist churches in the poverty-stricken countryside around Budapest and even further away to come and speak and lead Bible studies. Such meetings were often attended by local Jewish people. Mr. Miller felt I ought to continue the teaching and witnessing ministry the Lord had given me as long as possible. The plan was that I would base myself in Budapest and travel from the city to outlying churches, and in this way reach as many people at once as I could.

And so I began a time of difficult journeys for the Lord.

V

The People Multiply

DURING WARTIME, there are lines for everything: for food, for stamps, for newspapers, for medicine, and the longest lines of all are for tickets for trains. All the stations in Budapest were constantly jammed with people, searching, waiting, weeping, despairing beyond measure. With the address of a remote church in my handbag I would wait hours for a ticket, travel more hours in a packed train to an unfamiliar village, often walking miles until I found the church. Always in my arms I carried a heavy bundle of literature and my Bible.

Sometimes I was so exhausted and hungry when I arrived at the church I wanted only to rest. But always a large crowd of people would be waiting for me. I would begin to give my testimony and teach from the Word of God, and the Lord would greatly refresh me.

After the church meetings, I was anxious to go out into the streets to find Jewish homes to visit. Many of my people listened and accepted the literature I gave them. Some became angry and drove me away from their homes. I understood.

My small savings from the physiotherapy treatments were gone by this time. I had to depend on the inviting churches to pay for my train tickets. Often I went out with not a coin in my pocket, and I learned when I was very hungry and weak to ask my Heavenly Father for even my food; day by day, somehow, he provided it.

As the Nazi occupation spread over Europe like a great stain, fear intensified in Hungary, especially among the huge Jewish population. One could almost feel panic pulsing under the thin surface of daily life. In the Jewish villages people asked me what I had heard, what I knew, what other villages were doing, what I thought was going to happen.

How could I tell them? I lived in the same suffering. Felice had written me a grieving letter. Our doctor brother, Eugene, and his family had been transferred to a camp at Auschwitz. We were told that such camps were merely for the resettlement of Jews, but horrible stories were being circulated and denied—bizarre, grotesque, nightmare rumors that no one with a sane mind was able to believe. But something black and terrifying was swirling over our heads. None of us knew for sure what it was.

Yet some time as early as the summer before 1941, perhaps as early as May, history records that Hitler's police chief, Himmler, had secretly told his SS (*Schutz Staffeln*, Storm Troopers) that "the Führer had given the order for a 'final solution' of the Jewish question." The SS were to carry out his order.

It was a simple solution.

As I traveled back and forth from those milling, fearful villages, in crowded trains, tired and full of anxiety, my mind sometimes went back to the prewar days when I had been sculpting in Budapest. How we Hungarian students had read the newspapers from Germany with disbelief and disgust. To us then, Adolf Hitler was a fluke, a madman who would soon topple from his newfound power, to end his days as a lunatic.

Only a few people had read *Mein Kampf*. Most of us couldn't be bothered. We were disgusted by quotes from it. I remember Louis once laughing at a sentence from *Mein Kampf*. "With satanic joy in his face, the black-haired Jewish youth lurks in wait for the unsuspecting girl whom he defiles with his blood, thus stealing her from her people."

I had smiled at it too, but now, listening to the villagers' fears, phrases from *Mein Kampf* tormented me with anxiety for my gentle brother Eugene.

According to Hitler, we Jews were now officially vile and unclean. We had "unclean dress." We were at the heart of everything diseased. We controlled prostitution and white slave traffic. This vileness of our race resided in our blood. If Jews were alone in the world, we would stifle in our own filth.

In *Mein Kampf* Hitler taught that race was the central principle of all human existence. Since the beginning of time there had been two world adversaries, the Aryans and the Jews. The Aryans represented the perfection of human existence, the Jews the embodiment of evil.

"The Jews," Hitler had said, "were a ferment of decomposition." The vileness of the Jew he described as "so gigantic" that no one need be surprised if "among our [German] people the personification of the devil as the symbol of all evil assumes the living shape of the Jews.

"Two worlds face each other—the men of God and the men of Satan. The Jew is the anti-man, the creature of another god. *Wer kennt den Juden, kennt den Teufel!* [Whoever knows the Jew, knows the devil!]"

In wartime Hungary we fully understood that Hitler was eliminating all Jews from Germany. His purpose was to "cleanse" his Third Reich from every taint of the Jew. We felt the impact of the thousands of refugees massing at our borders, some escaping into the villages and forests of Hungary. Waves of human suffering swept first in one direction, only to be violently diverted to another course and then another—homeless, helpless, exhausted masses of people with nowhere to go. In Europe country after desperate country slammed its borders shut. Inside all occupied countries the "final solution" could not be hidden. Stories leaked out of deportations, thousands of Jews forced into slave labor, hundreds of thousands more "resettled." But where? Nobody knew.

In Hungary Jews had hope. Hungary had been precariously maintaining its neutral pro-German status. We prayed that the war would quickly end and the Allies would be victorious. Our Jewish children sang:

> Let's be joyous and tell our jokes.
> We'll hold a wake when Hitler chokes.

Or wanly jested:

What's the difference between the sun and Hitler? The sun goes down in the West and Hitler in the East.

A little rhyme counted up the enemies of Hitler and paid tribute to the Jewish underground:

Hitler won't be able to cope
With the English fleet
And the Russian sleet,
With American dollars
And Jewish smugglers.

Yet Hitler's "final solution" condemned Eugene and had already liquidated hundreds of thousands of defenseless Jews. It was a logical enough solution, a strategy straight from the deranged inferno of Hitler's mind: The empire of the Third Reich must be cleansed of every Jew. Hitler was the messenger of God for this immense task. It would be triumphantly accomplished by the mass transport of Jews to special camps throughout Europe. In the camps every Jewish man, woman, and child would be systematically liquidated. That was the "final solution."

But for me, in those last days of my missionary work in Budapest, I was not worried for myself. I had a Baptist work permit saying I was a Christian missionary and even permitting me to travel. And over that by far was the assurance that God was with me. It was not personal fear that drained me and made each day an ordeal. My heart was gripped with apprehension for my family, and the times themselves were overwhelming. The fabric of our Hungarian life was being savagely ripped apart by furious pro- and anti-Nazi factions, fanatical nationalists, corrupt opportunists, a wildly unstable government, and a populace locked in anxiety and confusion. I think in those days only the Jews were sure of anything—and that was the certainty of suffering.

This certainty drove me to share the gospel with as many Jews as I could. All were desperate for hope, and I had hope to give them. Everyone needed comfort, and I had comfort. In spite of fatigue, how could I stop my work? How could I not tell my people that Messiah had come, that our Deliverer was among us? My prayers for strength and God's guidance were anguished. But in the city there was increasing turmoil, and distractions and difficulties in getting in and out of Budapest increased every day.

Then it came to me that if I left Budapest and made my way northeast across Hungary to the Carpathian Mountains of Russia, I would pass through Jewish villages all along the way. I could travel and rest and teach and go on when weather and conditions permitted. I would not have to keep returning to Budapest.

I began this journey in the autumn of 1941, unprepared for what I saw. In 1938, the Munich Agreement (settling a crisis over the borders of Czechoslovakia) had given territory to Hungary, and in the transfer of lands Hungary added 250,000 Jews to its Jewish population of 400,000. As I traveled, I saw people in Jewish communities packed together in terrible conditions with little food. Their possessions had been left in their homelands or taken from them. By this time in Hungary, most Jews had been expelled from their jobs and thousands of men and boys had been taken to unknown places for forced labor. Gaunt faces of old men and women and children stared at me. But still they did not wear the yellow star.

Our nationalist Kállay government that had come to power in March 1941 valiantly refused Nazi demands that all Jews wear badges of identification and that all Hungarian Jews be deported *en masse* from Hungary to Nazi-occupied Poland. From Poland, our Jews would be "resettled." Kállay's argument was that he could not agree to Jewish resettlement so long as the Nazis were giving no satisfactory answer as to where the Jews were being resettled. So the Jews, those weak and old, lived on air and in fear in their wretched villages.

I was fervently thankful for any bit of food that was shared with me, for any corner of any room in which I could lie down at night, for any people who would listen to my Good News.

By the cold weather I had safely crossed the Hungarian border and entered Carpathian Russia at a small village that was also a trading center. This village was desperately overcrowded, but the people were glad to see a new face and I was able to witness. We were in the midst of a deep forest, and it was already very cold. Traveling was impossible, so I prepared myself to spend the winter among these primitive Carpathian Russian Jews. Almost everything that could be of use in the army had been cruelly stripped from the village by the Russian soldiers. Food, blankets, clothing, knives, axes—all were gone. Although we were in the middle of a forest, we had nothing for fuel.

Everyone wore layers of heavy clothing, but nothing kept out the constant terrible cold. Even in my own thick coat, I was bitterly cold day and night. Food here was scarce also, and I began to worry that my presence was depriving the village people of precious mouthfuls of nourishment.

Higher in the mountains, I heard, there was a Gentile peasant family living off by themselves. In an effort to spare the Jews, I went to visit this family. I was amazed—they were much better off than the villagers. Their wooden cottage was in a lovely part of the forest—and heated. Already it was snowing and so cold one's breath would actually freeze. They welcomed me and insisted I stay with them. There was no flour for bread, but there was corn and potatoes raised by the husband and wife. Most of their food was corn mixed with boiled potatoes, but they had milk and buttermilk from their cow. After so many months of hunger and exhaustion, the Lord brought me to a place where I could be warm and fed and could recover my strength.

In order to go to the village, one had to ski from one mountain to another. All my life I loved sports, so it was a pleasure for me to bundle up and ski to town for news or some small thing that was needed.

The family was Russian Orthodox and spoke Ukrainian, a language similar to High Russian. This was the first time I could really make use of the Slovak language I had been compelled to learn in my childhood days when Czechoslovakia took over our area. Then I had hated the Slovak lessons, but after I became a Christian I was thankful for every language I knew!

I had with me a Russian Bible. The woman in this tiny home was named Dosia, and unlike most she knew how to read. Almost all Russian villagers were illiterate, but Dosia had an old Russian Psalter which she read. According to the priests of the Russian Orthodox Church, only the Psalms could be read by lay people.

In the evenings by firelight, after all the work was done, she and I would sit down by the hearth and Dosia would eagerly read my Russian Bible as I read my Hungarian one. It was bitterly cold outside, perhaps fifteen degrees below zero. The logs in the fire would crackle loudly so that the noise sounded like an intruder smashing on the door. Her husband left us to study quietly together by the fire. So turbulent were our times it didn't strike us as odd that a Hungarian Jew would be warmed at the fire of a Russian Gentile, even though Hungarian soldiers were fighting with Germans against Russia during those very days Dosia and I were reading Scripture. When it happened that we got our hands on a newspaper, both of us grieved together at all the casualties, Hungarian and Russian, and we both prayed fervently for the defeat of the Third Reich.

Some evenings the sharp snapping of the logs on the fire sounded to me like the crack of a rifle discharge. I had heard stories of German Jews being herded together and shot over mass graves, and although I would not believe the stories, frightening pictures filled my imagination all the same. Eugene—Felice—Momma—I tried not to be afraid for them, but each one seemed to me to be particularly vulnerable in some way: Momma—frail and so alone in her old age; Felice—restricted by the needs of her little boys; Eugene—in Auschwitz; and my precious young brother Joseph, who had vanished.

Dosia listened to my fears with a stolid understanding. She had seen too much affliction in the passing of years to offer empty comfort. The suffering of her own Russian people had been very great. Together we concentrated ever more deeply on the Bibles on our laps.

One evening Dosia was reading aloud from Ephesians about the Lord Jesus loving the church and shedding His blood for it. Suddenly she stopped reading and exclaimed, "It is not the church, it is the blood of Jesus that saves!" Her face was as bright as the fire. It took only a few words of mine to lead Dosia to the Lord. She was so eager and so alive to spiritual truth that she blossomed into a radiant believer, overflowing with love and new joy.

Dosia became for me a picture of what can happen when a person comes into contact with the Bible. It seemed to me then, as it seems to me now, that the most important thing in the world is to bring God's Word to people.

Time passed slowly in that frozen world of forest and sky, but eventually ice began to drip and melt, and as the spring came I felt I ought to return to Budapest. The war news was conflicting, but one thing we dared to believe possible—perhaps the tide of Nazi success was being turned back. Certainly the forces of the German-Italian Axis were retreating from Africa. German troops had suffered terrible losses in the Russian winter and had been defeated at Stalingrad, according to the Russians. Could it be true? Was there a hope that my beloved Hungary might be spared Nazi occupation?

In Budapest I might be able to get news of Felice. Perhaps a letter from her was waiting, putting all my fear to rest. She might have had word from Eugene. I even imagined that Eugene might have been released from his camp by now and be looking for me in Budapest! Joseph might have turned up! In such times one hopes against hope. I knew perfectly well things were very bad for Jews in Felice's Slovakia and that Momma might be with Felice, subject to the same fate.

All the way back to Budapest I tried to fortify myself against disappointment by telling myself there would be no letter from Felice. But when I finally arrived in our beleaguered capital city, I raced through the streets, lugging my suitcase and apologizing to the people I bumped and pushed in my eagerness to get to the mission to see if there was any word. Nothing!

But I had no opportunity to brood. The American missionary Mary was there, as beautiful as before, although thinner than I had remembered her. Mary was astonished to hear that I had spent the winter in Carpathian Russia, near her area. (At this time the territory still belonged to Hungary.) Her eyes shone when I told her about Dosia and how I had witnessed in the Slovakian language and in broken Russian.

"Rose," Mary pleaded, "there are so many dear Christians who come to our meetings. They are very simple people and desperately need teaching. Our services are so crowded that sometimes our little oil lamp goes out because of lack of oxygen. Yet they will stay for hours if only they can learn the Word of God. You must come with me and help them."

There was nothing I wanted more. Mary promised I would have a cozy room in the orphanage, and I could help her with all the children as well. But still I did not feel at peace in my heart. I had been called to the Jews.

Mary saw my hesitation and understood. "Rose, we will have a pact. You will help me with all my dear Russians, and I will help you find Jewish people in the villages!"

In that long train journey from Budapest to the Russian mountains, I learned to love Mary. Her spirit was so steady and sweet and her goodness so transparent that she drew people to her everywhere she went. She had been born into a rich family in America, but had left everything that such a background had to offer her and had lived for years in the most primitive conditions among illiterate Russian peasants. She loved their children, the homeless, the sick, the abandoned, the orphans. The people were so devoted to her, they would follow her around just to touch her clothing and listen to her voice.

We arrived at Mary's orphanage late on a Saturday. Mary had arranged a spacious and clean room for me that I was to share with a dear Russian woman. After our exhausting journey, we were both ready for a long sleep. But Mary went immediately to work, so much had piled up in her absence. I was thinking of that bed and how good it would be to lie down when Mary announced that in the morning I was to preach at the Sunday morning service. I was aghast! I had never preached in Russian, and I was far too tired to try to prepare something.

But one didn't say no to Mary. Not even the strongest man could withstand a request from Mary. I knew she too was exhausted, but she gave herself immediately to the crowds of children eager to talk to her, and the workers with their urgent questions and problems. A strand of long blonde hair escaped from the bun at the back of her head. Mary tucked it behind her ears with a steady, patient hand.

How could I refuse? I ran to my room, leaving Mary in a sea of children blissful to have her back, the workers barking around the edges like so many seals clamoring for attention.

My fingers were shaking as I lit my little oil lamp and tried to put together my first message in Russian. How I prayed for the people who would have to listen to me, and how I prayed for a fluency that I knew I did not have.

And so on my first morning at the orphanage I had to stand up and speak, and the Lord truly helped me.

The village women wore black with black scarves on their

heads pulled forward and tied under their chins and behind their heads in the traditional Russian manner. As I gazed at their thin, weathered faces, my heart went out to them. I knew how much precious energy they had spent just to attend our little meeting.

The village priests, often as ignorant as the peasants, declared that Baptists were heretics and told the people they were forbidden to come to the services or even speak to Mary or anyone at the orphanage. But they came anyway, and many of them were terribly persecuted.

On the train Mary had told me about one new believer, a woman called Nadezda, who asked to be baptized in the stream that ran down the mountain just behind the orphanage. Her husband had been furious. "If you dare to be baptized," he promised her, "I will kill you on the spot with an axe." Nadezda was very frightened and postponed her baptism for a time. But finally she couldn't wait any longer. She was determined to follow the Lord in baptism, and so Mary set a date and all the believers began to pray.

When the day of baptism arrived, Nadezda came to the stream along with some others who were being baptized. Shortly before the service, her husband came crashing through the trees, axe in hand, livid with rage. Nadezda went as white as her baptismal robe. She truly believed she was going to her death, and although she was shaking she stepped into the water all the same. When her husband saw her courage and the praying of all the people, he suddenly threw the axe down and plunged weeping into the stream after her. He accepted the Lord in that icy water and was baptized together with his wife.

Not all the stories of persecution ended like Nadezda's, however, and many in those Orthodox villages had to suffer much for their faith. They were denied burial, often beaten, driven off from the fields, their children bullied and ostracized. Sometimes their wretched little cottages were vandalized or burned.

The people were so poor that anywhere they went, no matter how long a journey they had to walk and none of them had shoes. Even in the dead of winter, when the snow was deep and the ground covered with ice, they had only rags or bark to cover their feet, and many didn't even bother with rags.

I learned to walk in those mountains, sometimes traveling five or six miles one way to get something or make a visit—and in all kinds of weather. Mary walked too. The orphanage did have one antique bicycle, but it was almost always in use by somebody, and it was like Mary to let others use it. Mary's quiet authority at the orphanage was never questioned. Everyone knew that when Mary said something, she meant it. She meant it for herself, but everyone was included.

Our orphanage became more packed with children every day, and there was no room for workers and visitors and the many people who came wanting rest or some food or a place to sleep. Miraculously money came from America, and Mary was determined to build a new, bigger orphanage even though the war was going on and it was impossible to get anything.

The project of building the new orphanage became very precious to all the village. Everyone helped. Mary herself labored all day like a man, and all the children worked alongside of her. She never spared herself from any hard work and never needed to order anyone to do anything. People just followed her example, and she taught that there is joy in doing anything for the Lord.

No matter what Mary did, devotions always came first—whether it was harvesting or building or whatever. The children loved to listen to her; they called her "Mamochka" (Russian for "Mother"), and she had raised many of them from babyhood to their teens.

No one got up earlier than Mary, and she saw everyone to bed. I remember at two o'clock in the morning she would still be sitting at her desk, typing letters in the flickering light of her little oil lamp. When she finally made her way to bed, she would walk through the children's rooms, covering up the little ones, making sure all were contented and sleeping.

One day I was traveling back to the orphanage from a distant village when I saw a strange sight. A *gendarme* was leading an exhausted group of young children along the road. Each child carried a yellow bag of the same size. When I caught up to them I saw that the children appeared to be Jewish.

"Excuse me, who are these children, please, and where are they going?" I tried to be unusually polite because it was always difficult to tell whether *gendarmes* would be kindly or hostile.

This officer was friendly, and he replied that they were Jewish

Hungarian children who had escaped illegally with their parents into Communist Russia. Inside Russia, the children had been torn away from their parents and put in an orphanage.

Knowing the Nazi army was advancing deep into Russia, a teacher there had secretly taken the children to the Hungarian border and let them cross, thinking as Jews they would be safer in Hungary. They had been caught, the guard explained, and had to be returned to Russia.

The officer gave me his address in the next city, and I raced to our orphanage to tell Mary. Mary's face went suddenly white. She ran to her desk and pulled out a lot of money. Perhaps she gave me all she had. "Hurry, Rose! Go after the children and bring them back! We will make room for them here."

When I reached the town I found the *gendarme*, and he and his wife very kindly invited me into their home and gave me lodging. The children had been taken to be interrogated. In the town was a castle that had been turned into a prison for people accused of being spies. I was shocked that the children had been admitted to this prison, because it was a notorious place where terrible things were done.

The officer urged me not to go to the prison, but to wait to see what would be done. He thought if I went myself, I would be arrested and locked up.

I had to find the children. It was difficult to get in and the guards treated me very roughly, but finally I was allowed to enter. The place was worse than the stories I had heard about it, and I saw things that horrified me. I was distraught with worry for these little children, some not more than five years old. Finally I discovered that they were being released, but would have to walk all the way to the border of Russia.

For several days I walked with those children and bought them food at markets along the way. When their soldier guards stopped for the night, I was allowed to cook them food. Some people in the villages where we stopped offered to help me because they pitied the children. I was even allowed to carry a few of them to local doctors, because their feet were bleeding from days of walking.

Finally we came to a large city in the district, and the children were taken to a huge prison. I was forced to remain outside. I wept and pled with the *gendarmes*. I offered all the money I had. I promised to bring more—as much as they wanted. I would do anything, but those tiny children were taken inside the prison, still clutching tightly their little yellow bags. From there I knew they would go to the Nazi camps in Russia.

I returned to the orphanage brokenhearted. My concern for my mother greatly increased after this experience. She was still living in Piešťany, long since annexed to Czechoslovakia. In 1939 the Germans had occupied Czechoslovakia, but since September of 1941, all Jews in the country were required to wear the identifying yellow Star of David, making them liable to forced labor, eviction from specified towns and districts, and deportation.

Although Felice and her husband and little boys were in enormous danger in Slovakia, they were very active Christian believers by this time. None of the children in our family looked Jewish, so the Nazis took Felice and her family to be Gentiles.

Felice eventually managed to have mother with her, but things were becoming so bad that Felice was terrified that mother would be discovered and taken away and that in the process disaster would fall upon them all. Felice had been hiding mother and had paid a considerable sum of money to do it, but the Nazis were searching everywhere for Jews, dragging them out of hiding, throwing them on trucks for transport to the camps. Rabbis, children, old people, babies—there was mercy for no one, or anyone who hid Jews.

Felice thought mother would be safer in Hungary, but how could I explain from the orphanage that I myself had no money or food, that I was traveling every day, that I had no place to hide her and no money to feed her?

In spite of my anxiety, I continued my missionary journeys, traveling long miles by foot to the withered Jewish villages that once flourished in the Carpathian Mountains. Sometimes a church in a city would send me a train ticket to come and speak and thus I would be able to visit places too distant for walking.

In January 1942 I found myself on a crowded train that pulled itself wearily through the frozen countryside. I was on my way to a church, and in my suitcase were tracts in all the languages of Europe.

There were always Jews on the trains and I sought them out,

trying to sit with them and beginning conversations so I could witness. Often they were frightened, trying to flee somewhere or find a loved one. Usually they didn't want to talk or be conspicuous in any way.

But on this day I was able to meet two Jews who were carrying on a whispered conversation in Yiddish. Since I could speak Yiddish, I began talking with them, telling them about Jesus, the Jewish Messiah. We were engrossed in conversation. I did not see the military officer in the crowded compartment until his hand fell on my shoulder.

"It is forbidden to pass out political literature," he charged. "You are under arrest."

It is true I had tried to give tracts in Yiddish to my Jewish acquaintances. My suitcase was full of literature, and the officer had seen it. It was no use protesting I was a missionary and the contents of my suitcase was Christian literature and Bibles. It was enough to be conferring with Jews.

I was pulled off the train at the next stop and taken to a prison. The next few hours were a confusion of crowds, interrogations, orders, being rushed from one office and prison to another.

After a long march with many others over the shocked and silent countryside, I was thrust through the gates of a huge prison. To my horror it was the same prison from which I had had to part from the band of dear little children who had been forced into Russia.

Thousands of people were being held there. My coat was taken away from me, and I was locked in a cell with an iron door. The only food I received was an unpeeled boiled potato and a jug of water. In the corner of the cell was an open toilet. There was almost no light and no air. My suitcase had been taken away by the guards, but they had allowed me to keep my Bible.

It was a wretched place and very, very cold, but I rejoiced that I could suffer for serving my Lord. I passed the time praying and reading, and it was a long time. When I was finally taken for interrogation, the detectives knew all about me, and they found fault with everything. In my suitcase were tracts that had been printed in America. They accused me of being a spy because Hungary was at war with America by this time. On my identification card my profession was stated as a "private teacher" because I had a diploma for physical education. That was my last paying job. But the interrogators thought that this was just a cover-up for being a spy.

They had also found out that I had been in England in 1937, and that confirmed their suspicions. My connection with Mary, an American, was held against me. All my traveling was held against me. My passport was no longer valid, and it was not possible for me to get a new one; so I had removed my picture from the document, hoping I could use the photo for new papers. When they found the passport without a picture, they were absolutely convinced that they had a spy!

The questioning went on for hours, and sometimes I was led to different rooms where I passed people in horrifying conditions, shackled in huge chains as thick as my arm.

I had been a Christian less than two years, but I was greatly looking forward to seeing the Lord. I was absolutely sure I would be killed, and the Lord's presence with me was so real I was joyful and full of peace.

One day in the cell I began to feel very ill from lack of air. There was a little window in the iron door, but it was only opened when they passed in food. I began to sing and pray; I was becoming desperate for air. I didn't know there was a *gendarme* standing on the other side of the door. When he heard me, he opened the door and looked in at me.

"Aren't you afraid of the dark?"

"No." I gulped in the fresh air and was able to gasp, "The Lord Jesus is my light."

As he asked me several questions, the oxygen greatly revived me. He listened to me intently until he was angrily called away by another guard. As he closed the door he seemed bemused. The last I saw of daylight was him shaking his head. "Strange, I never saw a prisoner like you." I sank down on the floor of my cell in tears of gratitude to God. I could breathe again, although I tried to take shallow breaths to conserve oxygen.

The next time I was taken to interrogation, the *gendarmes* began to ask me questions I had no idea how to answer. They wanted to know about international spy rings and what were the names of the men in charge in the various cities of Europe, especially London, where they seemed to feel I had made my initial contacts. When I couldn't answer, they threatened me terribly and asked how I expected to be able to stand against the invincible might of the SS. I could only think of Scripture and so I told them, "I am well content with weaknesses, with insults, with distresses, with persecutions, with difficulties for Christ's sake; for when I am weak, then I am strong."

Of course, they became very angry with me because I was not helping them with the information they wanted. The officer in charge had cruelly polished boots with sharp riding spurs on them. He crashed his foot down on the floor and many times assured me that he had the power to kill me instantly if I did not answer.

I was quite sure I was going to meet my death in that prison. His words only encouraged me. After so long a time of questioning without rest or food or water, I felt reality slipping away. Scripture poured into my head, and I could think of nothing to say except the verses that the questions triggered in my mind. When the death threats became relentless and the *gendarmes* began to be abusive, I gasped, "Truly, truly, I say to you, he who hears My Word, and believes Him who sent Me, has eternal life, and does not come into judgment, but has passed out of death into life."

Finally the fury of the *gendarmes* suddenly subsided. The officer lit a cigarette and looked at me coldly with a shrug. "Well, you couldn't have sucked these answers out of your little finger," he spat out as he turned away. So I was taken away, not to solitary confinement where I had been but to a huge cell full of Jews. Their "crime" was that they had escaped from Poland or Czechoslovakia where they had already been arrested. Now they were to be sent to the camps.

We women were in a room without a door, sleeping on bare boards. There was no covering, and the *gendarmes* had taken away my coat. But I still had my Bible, and I was able to witness to the Jewish people there, both men and women.

It was not the terrible cold that I found so hard to bear. For the first time in my life I had lice. The suffering that these tiny, bloodsucking insects cause is indescribable. Only people confined closely together for long periods of time can understand the horror that accompanies the infestation of lice. It is not only that the saliva of lice leaves intense itching after the insect has bitten its victim; often infection and serum sickness are caused by the insects, so that people heavily infested develop high fevers, scalding rashes, even aching in the bones and joints, as well as swelling in the lymph glands throughout the body. For those in a weakened condition, lice can be fatal.

The prison officials spent a good deal of time disinfecting people's clothing, but it was impossible to control the lice, and misery was endemic.

While I was in that Hungarian prison I had another initiation into horror, although it was softened at the time because I simply did not believe what I was told.

In the men's prison was a small Jewish boy of eight years old, who stayed close to the side of a man whom I at first took to be his father. Later I understood that the boy's real father had died in a concentration camp in Poland, but the boy had escaped and had attached himself to the kind man to whom he clung.

The boy had been in a labor concentration camp, Majdanek, near Lublin in Poland. This camp had been set up in 1940 for slave labor. It was about this camp that the little boy raved. He told us, "They are making soap out of our people!" He tried to describe what had happened to his father when they had arrived —how his father had been ordered to undress, how police wielding whips and stocks had hurried him along to "shower rooms." He talked wildly about the fires, about the smoke and the smell. We tried to comfort him, certain that the loss of his father had deranged his mind.

I was in that prison for several more days. In spite of the terror of that place, I was detached from it because I felt that I would be killed. I was thankful that the Lord had put me in such a place and made it possible for me to witness to suffering people in the last hours I had on earth.

One morning I was pulled out of the press of prisoners in our cell and commanded to leave. I was free! My belongings were returned to me with the order that I must never return to that district of Carpathian Russia where I had been ministering. I had to return immediately to my own city. In a daze I made my way back to Budapest, eventually to stay for a while in the home of a kind Christian medical doctor and his family who lived on the west side of the Danube River.

For a long time I was in terrible agony. All the stories I had heard about what happened to Jews filled my mind. I pictured mother on those trucks, in the camps. I felt I *had* to bring her to Hungary, but when I tried to plan where I might hide her, what I might do with her, my mind almost exploded with panic. Her presence would be fatal to any Gentile family who would take her in. There was no one I could ask. She was seventy-four years old. How could she travel safely in the first place? And in Hungary, swollen with refugees, where could I find a place for her?

Months later I was reading in *Daily Light*. It was August 14, 1942. The first verse that day was, "The joy of the Lord is your strength." I cried out to God, "Lord, You know I am in such grief. My own mother is in danger of being taken to the camps. How can I rejoice in You when she is in such a terrible situation and I don't know any way out?"

I struggled with God on that sweltering morning in my tiny room. Every bit of my willful spirit raged helplessly against trusting the Lord and rejoicing in Him when I was in such anguish for my mother. Finally I was quiet enough to remember something Mr. Miller told me in the very beginning of my Christian life. "Rose, if the Lord tells us something is white but we think it is black, we just have to accept that it is white."

The last verse of the reading said, "I will joy in the God of my salvation." The Lord told me to trust in Him and to rejoice in Him in spite of agony and sorrow.

When I got up from my knees, I wrote my sister and told her I was not able to take mother simply because I had no home myself and mother would be physically unable to travel with me. I told Felice we had to trust in the Lord and leave mother in His hands. When I had finally accepted the circumstances and written the letter, I had release from the awful anguish. I was able to "joy in the Lord." As long as I kept my mind and heart fixed on Him, I was able to bear the situation.

It was during this time that I received a message that my youngest brother, Joseph, had been taken on a transport to Auschwitz. So many terrible stories were engulfing Europe by this time that my mind refused to accept the news. Nothing could happen to him! I could almost feel his baby hand clutching mine as the two of us ran across the childhood gardens of Piešťany.

I saw us at the synagogue in the women's gallery with Momma, teasing mother until she let us slip outside to play. I remembered Joseph in his first grown-up suit, standing shyly before Poppa and us all, blushing at our admiration. Joseph! Something in my heart shifted as I thought of him. *Nothing could happen to Joseph!* I felt a terrible determination to live, to keep on going, as if as long as my own life continued it would be impossible for Joseph's to end.

Somehow I kept traveling back and forth from Budapest to the countryside, ministering in any church that would invite me, looking always for the Jewish communities where I could spend time talking and giving out literature. I didn't try to get a job—it would have been impossible for me as a Jew—and I wanted to spend all my time witnessing and serving the Lord.

Actually, Jewish or not, nobody wanted a physiotherapist in those terrible times. It is a curious thing, but people hardly ever even went to a doctor. And the practice of psychiatry, begun in Vienna by Dr. Sigmund Freud, which had begun to flourish before the war, completely fell off. There was so much trouble in the world, a little ache or pain, a little worry, a fever was hardly noticed. And besides, most doctors had been taken to the front. Very few were left for civilian practice, and I don't think people minded that shortage at all.

I had had a sheltered and pampered childhood in Piešťany. My youth had been spent in self-indulgence. I had always been terribly fastidious about what food I ate and how I was dressed. I wanted to exude health and beauty. I associated only with the most cultured, most educated, most artistic and "interesting" people. I was to be a great dancer or a great sculptor, and I wanted everyone to know it and believe it. How imperious I had been!

In those last days in Budapest I used to reflect on how lowly I had become. My clothes were shabby and my shoes in pieces. I was often hungry. Most of the people I spent my time with were illiterate and had barely traveled outside their own villages. Yet I was happy doing the Lord's work and happy that I could live humbly as He had.

How little I knew of what was to come and that those days of cold and poverty and hunger would soon seem like heavenly bliss to me.

But the Lord had more to teach me. One day in Budapest a businessman came to me and asked if I would like to come to his town and minister there. Winter was coming on, and I was very weary and cold. I wanted a place where I could stay put for the bitter weather and still carry on with my missionary work. When he told me his town had a huge Jewish population, I was eager to go.

After staying with different families, I was finally offered a place of my own with a supposedly Christian family. It was not a happy home. The man was continually finding fault with everyone, but never with himself. That home had the typical tiny cellar room used to store vegetables for the whole winter, plus a stove where water was boiled and the laundry could be done. It was there that I lived. Because I had no money at all, I offered to clean the house in exchange for the room, and this seemed an agreeable arrangement to the family.

The room was so small that my head touched the ceiling. The floor was mud, and the rusty iron bed took up all the space. For light there was a slit of a window through which I could see the feet of people passing by on the road. I painted the bed silver, hung some Scripture posters on the wall, and found myself to be quite content. With the last bit of money I bought potatoes and onions.

I once read a novel about a medical student in Egypt. During his student days he was very poor, and all he had to eat were onions. He was very brave and said simply, "One can keep alive!" When I looked at that modest bundle of potatoes and onions that was all I had to eat for the winter, I remembered that story and I said, "Well, as long as they last— one can keep alive!" I'm glad the thought didn't occur to me that what I had read was fiction!

Everything was rationed and almost impossible to get even with the coupons, but that was another worry I did not have. It was not permitted for me to get coupons, because I was a Jew. If I tried to register, I would have been taken for labor or worse. Sometimes I wished I did have coupons because the sights on the streets were terrible. I thought if I only had some food myself, I could give it to the people I saw.

Once I came upon a large group of soldiers lying by the roadside with frozen hands and feet. Perhaps they were waiting to be transported to a hospital. Nobody knew why they were there. There were so many of them, I think people were afraid that if they tried to help they would lose what little they had to keep themselves alive.

I had nothing to give, so I wasn't afraid. I went to the Baptist church and started collecting a tiny bit of food from each person there. Some gave me a teaspoon or two of flour, some a bit of oil, and gradually I had enough to bake biscuits for the men.

There was so much one could do in those days because the towns, hospitals, and clinics were crowded with people. I tried to visit the hospitals and give out tracts and Gospels when I could get in. Everything was mixed up, and sometimes there were civilians and soldiers in the same hospital. During my visits to a hospital, I made friends with a Jewess who was dying of tuberculosis. Her eyes were huge in her thin face, and she was greatly wasted from the disease. The first time I saw her her two little daughters were at her bedside, watching her fearfully. Her husband had been taken into the army, and those two little children were quite alone.

I went to their home and started taking care of them. They had absolutely nothing—not even clothes to wear. I didn't know anything about sewing, but I had a dress that I cut up to make two little dresses for them. The Lord must have done the sewing for me! There were dear Christian women in that neighborhood, and they gave me food for the little girls. One would bring an egg, another some flour, another half a cup of oil. To this I added a potato or onion from my little bag, and so the Lord kept me alive as well as the two dear girls.

The mother allowed me to teach the children the Bible. Their apartment opened onto a courtyard where there were many little flats, all belonging to Jews, sharing the same winter view of a bare, scraggly tree. It was a sad place. The men were gone, taken to labor camps or the army, or often no one knew where. The women were fairly young, with little children, and they were desperate in their loneliness and fear. When they saw my devotion toward the two girls and how I, a stranger, was mothering them, they were astonished. Soon some of them came to the Bible classes I conducted for the children.

The women's hearts were wounded. They were tender and

open and didn't object when I told them about the loving Savior Who wanted to be their Messiah. My two little girls quickly accepted the Lord, and when their mother was well enough to come home she too became a believer. Others followed, and it was a marvelous time for me in the Lord's service. Although we all were very poor, I was rich in the Lord, and He was comforting me.

In the early spring a pastor came to see me. He was responsible for fourteen churches, and because he could not possibly serve such a large number of congregations every Sunday, he asked me to hold Sunday services in some of them, even though I was a woman. There were many Jewish people in the areas where his Baptist churches were, so I agreed and began to travel again, conducting meetings and visiting the barren villages.

It was very difficult to get accurate news of what was happening in the war. Rumors were thick, and the position of Hungary in Europe grew more and more dangerous as Hitler's armies increasingly suffered defeats. Hungary had joined with Germany on paper as early as November 1940 in the Tripartite Pact. This was an agreement signed originally by Germany, Italy, and Japan, in which each power promised to assist the other if one of them was attacked by a country not already in the war. Many other European countries eventually signed the Pact on Hitler's insistence. In April of 1941, the Hungarian army occupied a part of Yugoslavia, and in June joined German forces in invading Russia.

But all the while, Hungary's participation with the Germans was less than wholehearted. Our Regent, Nicholas Horthy, resisted German demands for Hungary's general mobilization. Our government was desperately trying to disentangle Hungary from the war. As many Hungarian troops as possible were recalled from the front. What we wanted, of course, was to remain neutral. It would have been suicide to fight against Germany, but there was little love for the Third Reich among most Hungarians, who wanted Hungary to belong to Hungary.

One of our great national heroes was a poet and patriot, Sandor Petofi, who was killed at twenty-seven in the Hungarian War for Freedom (against the Habsburgs) in 1849. Petofi came to be a legendary figure in our history, symbolizing our struggle for national liberty. His handsome face with his curly black hair and sweeping romantic moustache can be found all over Hungary, in the company of angels and Muses, in pictures on the walls of country inns.

His poem "Up Hungarians!" was the rallying cry for all patriots of all wars. I had heard it first as a tiny child. Now, when it was sung or recited in Hungary in the forties, it was not to rouse support for the Third Reich!

> *Up, Hungarians! It's your country calling!*
> *Now's the moment, now or never!*
> *Shall we be slaves? Shall we be free?*
> *That's the question—what's your answer?*
> *In God's great Name, we swear, we swear,*
> *No more shall we be slaves—no more!*

It is not surprising then that in early 1944, even as I was trudging back and forth across the bleak countryside helping with the fourteen churches, Hitler's fury was turned against Hungary. The Axis had already suffered terrible losses in Africa, according to people who managed to listen to shortwave broadcasts from the Allies. Could it be true?

"Hungary," Hitler raged, "is acting more like a neutral than a German ally." So in that trembling spring of 1944, Hitler summoned our Regent Horthy and his cabinet to a meeting in Germany and confronted Horthy with Hungary's "treachery." He declared that Germany had to occupy Hungary. When our officials returned to Budapest the next day, the German occupation of Hungary had already been completed.

We had no idea of the stunning losses that Germany had suffered. We were terrified by the Third Reich and by the arrival again in Hungary, on March 19, of the high German official Adolf Eichmann. Ten days later, new and more severe anti-Jewish laws were enacted. Factories and shops and business places belonging to Jews were confiscated. Jewish people had to wear the yellow Star of David with the inscription in the center, "A Jew." Jews were herded into special areas for deportation to camps outside of Hungary.

I still had papers from the Baptist church, so I was not compelled to wear the Star of David. I actually never wore it. But the secret police were watching me. They hadn't given up the idea that I was a spy. Once they came to the house in the town of Beregovo in which I had a room and searched through all my belongings. They even turned my typewriter upside down, looking for secret letters or some coding apparatus. They found nothing. My landlady was angry and fearful, and even though she belonged to a church, she forced me to leave. I found a very humble peasant woman and her daughter who were willing to take me in. So I stayed with them until the end.

As much as possible I continued to attend prayer meetings and to witness to Jewish people in the town, but horror had fallen upon everyone, and week by week thousands of Jews from all over Hungary were brought into the city for transport. Often huge crowds of Jews would be crammed in the synagogue, waiting for the transport trucks, or marched from the synagogue to the railroads where they would be forced into boxcars. They arrived in our town staggering and exhausted, some in little carts pulled by frothing horses. Little children and old people and weeping mothers. They had almost nothing with them. I had never seen such sad, hopeless faces.

It was a terrible scene, and I watched weeping and praying and so burdened for them all I could hardly breathe. Then a shock went through my body. I recognized some of the villagers with whom I had lived and worked and witnessed. Some of them were my friends. I longed to be with them. If they were to be starved, I wanted to starve. If they were being taken over the border to be killed, I wanted to be killed with them. I felt I belonged to them; I was one with them; I was their teacher. I was the only one who could bring them the Word of God in their anguish. I had promised God I would be his witness to them.

But how often in my life had I impulsively jumped into something, only to bring disaster upon myself! My childish war against learning Czechoslovakian had caused me so much wretchedness as a little schoolgirl. My determination to be a great dancer, a great sculptor, my enthusiasm for the Gnostics, my joining the spiritist groups, my marriage to Louis . . . what grief my spontaneity had caused me.

Now I stumbled through the streets of Beregovo with a bursting heart. I didn't know if my longing to be with my Jewish people was a response of my own grief, or if it was the direction of the Lord. If it was only from the depths of my own being—my guilt at being free, my grieving for Eugene and Joseph, my remorse at not being able to help mother, and my inability to witness to my beloved Jewish villagers who were already being deported—then I knew I could not face what would be ahead. But if the Lord was sending me, I knew also I would receive His strength and grace for whatever came.

It seemed wise to consult with friends, two Christian pastors at the Baptist church. "Rose!" the oldest of them gasped, pushing his hand through his thick black hair. "What are you thinking of? We need you desperately in the work here. How can you say you love us if you talk about going with the Jewish people? You will die and be gone!"

The other church officer was a pale, worn-looking brother. His eyes filled with tears. "Many of us believe that the church is now going through the Tribulation."

I nodded. It was hard to imagine anything worse than what was happening. Perhaps the Tribulation had begun. Certainly Hitler could be the Antichrist.

"The Christians need you. You must leave the Jews to God. The Body of Christ groans in travail. You must help us minister while there is yet time."

We prayed desperately, pleading for the will of God. My own spirit was in anguish, pulled in two directions. Yet even as we prayed I could hear the transport trucks rolling through the streets under our window.

It was a terrible month of conflict for me. I began to realize how much I would endanger others willing to shelter me and help me and give me food and money if I made myself known as a Jew. I began writing letters to my friends and my family, telling them not to write to me anymore. I had not heard from Felice or my mother in a long time. I forced myself to believe they were safe and wrote them not to try to contact me.

One of my friends was Mrs. Wasserzug, a wonderfully lively and intelligent woman who was head of a Bible school in Switzerland. When she received my farewell letter, she wrote me immediately and urged me to go illegally to Switzerland to join her and her husband. There was a plan already made for it, but I was certain that this was not the Lord's will. How could I run away?

I was fasting and praying and reading the Bible. Day by day friends of mine were rounded up and taken to the places in Beregovo where Jews were assembled for transport. I was able to take some food for them. Even though they were very hungry, they didn't want me to come. They pushed me away and told me to hide. Often they pretended not to know me.

The peasant woman with whom I was staying stopped me one day in the doorway of my room and gave me a black kerchief to wear. It was customary in Hungary and in the neighboring countries for women to wear black dresses and black scarves on their heads. I had not followed this peasant custom, but my friend was apprehensive about my safety. She pleaded with me to be as inconspicuous as possible, so I took the black kerchief gratefully.

We went inside my room and began to discuss the situation. She was a God-fearing woman who loved the Lord with all her heart, and she loved the Jewish people. She was in very great danger because I was living in her house. Anyone who sheltered a Jew would suffer the same fate as a Jew. But she was not thinking of her own safety—only of mine. She asked me to read Psalm 80 with her. Many years have passed, but I can never read this Psalm without remembering her and seeing her in my room as we wept and read the Psalm together. As we read the verses aloud, the terrifying two-tone sirens of the Nazi police vans patrolling the streets of the town drowned out the words.

> Oh give ear, Shepherd of Israel, Thou who dost lead Joseph like a flock; Thou who art enthroned above the cherubim, shine forth! Before Ephraim and Benjamin and Manasseh, stir up Thy power, and come to save us!
>
> O God, restore us, and cause Thy face to shine upon us, and we will be saved. O Lord God of hosts, how long wilt Thou be angry with the prayer of Thy people? Thou hast fed them with the bread of tears, and Thou hast made them to drink tears in large measure. Thou dost make us an object of contention to our neighbors; and our enemies laugh among themselves.
>
> O God of hosts, restore us, and cause Thy face to shine upon us, and we will be saved. Thou didst remove a vine from Egypt; Thou

didst drive out the nations, and didst plant it. Thou didst clear the ground before it, and it took deep root and filled the land. The mountains were covered with its shadow; and the cedars of God with its boughs. It was sending out its branches to the sea, and its shoots to the River. Why hast Thou broken down its hedges, so that all who pass that way pick its fruit? A boar from the forest eats it away, and whatever moves in the field feeds on it.

The old peasant woman reached over and grasped my hands. Our tears were falling and ran together over our tightly intertwined fingers. In a single whisper we read aloud the end of the Psalm:

O God of hosts, turn again now, we beseech Thee. Look down from heaven and see, and take care of this vine, even the shoot which Thy right hand has planted. And on the son whom Thou hast strengthened for Thyself. It is burned with fire, it is cut down; They perish at the rebuke of Thy countenance. Let Thy hand be upon the man of Thy right hand, upon the son of man whom Thou didst make strong for Thyself. Then we shall not turn back from Thee; Revive us, and we will call upon Thy name.

O Lord God of hosts, restore us; Cause Thy face to shine upon us, and we will be saved.

"Perhaps the Nazis are transporting Jews to Palestine," I had suggested to my pastor friends. How I longed that this might be true! "If they are going to Palestine, then I want to go with them." But both pastors had shaken their heads vehemently. "No! Dear Rose! There is an easier way to go to Palestine!"

Well, the Lord knew better. For me there was no easier way. There was peace in my heart when I got up from my knees that day in that room. Somehow I knew I no longer needed to fast and pray and seek the will of the Lord. I went out of the room and into the street.

And so it happened—the Lord decided for me. I was taken in the street to be with my people.

VI

Agony
and Slavery

I WAS PERMITTED TO RETURN to my room and
gather a few things. I thought perhaps the Nazis
would transport us into the countryside and
leave us to starve. I remember gathering my
best clothes (such as they were) and bedding. I was
allowed to take a mattress to sleep on. I took as many
Bibles as I could carry—my large Hebrew Bible for witnessing,
and some in different languages. I rushed staggering through the
streets of Beregovo, bent over from the load on my back. As I
made my way to the transport center, people averted their eyes or
shouted, "Good riddance!" I was blissfully at peace, knowing
that the Lord had chosen my lot for me.

We were packed into transport cars and traveled a surprisingly
short distance to a vacant brick factory outside Beregovo. Already
it was filled with Jews. Great masses of people huddled in the
buildings that sprawled along the tracks where trains had once
unloaded raw materials and loaded bricks.

I was overjoyed to find, in all that mass of humanity, friends
from the remote villages where I had traveled and even some Jews
who had made professions of faith in Jesus as Messiah. One
woman was an old friend from a very distant village—a mother of
two tiny children, whose seraphic faces were already badly bitten

by lice. Her husband had already been taken to the camps. I put my mattress next to hers. There was part of a roof over our heads and a section of wall to lean against. It was the spring of 1944 and not very cold.

While we were in that factory many would come to me and ask about their destiny. I read them prophecies from Scripture, and I constantly assured them that God had not forsaken Israel, that He had an everlasting purpose for her. Over and over I pleaded with them to give their hearts to the Lord and to turn to Him. People were tenderhearted and receptive, and I blessed God that in all their suffering He sent them a witness, even if it was only me. The people were oppressed with fear and tormented with anxiety and hope. They so wanted to live, naturally. Every human being wants to live.

Condemned, but to what? Thousands of us formed a desolate community of suffering, waiting day after day, simply waiting, but for what? Old people with empty eyes stared into the air in front of them, not seeing the madness around them—the quarrels, the indecencies, the angelic babies with inscrutable staring faces, the distraught mothers, the silent, terrified children.

We were not permitted for an instant to leave the inside of the building. Not a fragment of sky or field could be seen, not a muscle exercised except for the difficult trek over bodies to the halls that were used as toilets. These halls were places of unspeakable scenes, and yet even the children had to go there.

Still people spoke with mustered hope that things might not be so bad. We were, after all, on the outskirts of Beregovo, and that was a good sign. We had not been loaded into transport trains like so many thousands of others. Perhaps we would be sent to work in the factories of Hungary! I looked across the expanse of humanity on the brick factory floor—the glistening, luxuriant carpet of children's heads, the sea of dark kerchiefs of the old—and said nothing.

One morning we were aroused from our fitful dozing by a sound that shot terror into every one of us—the faint sound of an approaching train that grew thunderously loud as it ground and bumped to a halt alongside the factory. We could smell iron against iron as the wheels braked against the sections of track. *Gendarmes* streamed into the building, shouting repeatedly that everyone must be searched. There was frantic confusion. Everybody scrambled to gather up their carefully hoarded possessions and to rush outside in obedience to the *gendarmes'* demands.

All valuables had to be given up. People tore off their watches and rings, flung down their money and jewelry until fabulous piles of riches were stacked on the Gestapo tables. I had nothing, so I waited rather anxiously, not wanting to appear uncooperative as to what I should do or where I should go. In moments there was another order: females were to strip! The *gendarmes* would ensure that the secret places of the body were not used to hide jewels. Many women fainted and were beaten back to consciousness. Horror filled us all. But to search so many hundreds of women took time, and before it was my turn the cattle cars were already so tightly packed with their shocked and bleeding victims that there was no room for anyone else. Hundreds of us, paralyzed with terror, were forced back into the brick factory to fall upon the disarray of mattresses and scattered possessions.

The Lord is my Shepherd. *Everyone must be searched!* I shall not want. *All valuables and money on the tables!* He makes me to lie down in green pastures. *All females are to strip!* He restores my soul. *Get up or you will be killed!* He leads me in the paths of righteousness. *Onto the train! Move! Move!* Yea, though I walk through the valley of death . . . The screaming of children filled my ears. I tried to shut out the utter horror on their faces and the abyss of memories that churned in my mind.

Oddly, I had a valuable gold fountain pen in my pocket. In the panic of the search, I had forgotten it. After a time I took a piece of paper and wrote a message to the pastors in Budapest. On it I wrote: "I am alive and not ill. I am able to witness and am at peace." I don't think my suffering was any less than the others with me, but I wanted in some way to express the inexpressible: in the midst of the horror—Jesus was there. I gave the fountain pen to a guard and asked him to get the message out for me.

A week after the first transport, the trains came again. There was consternation far greater than the first panic seven days before. Everything was repeated in exactly the same order as before. I was shaking violently, as if from the most bitter cold, although the pale spring sun shone on our white and shrinking flesh. In the frenzy of the shouting, the brutal clubbing of defenseless masses

111

of people, the rushing of lines, helped along by dogs and rifle butts, I hardly realized what I was doing. I clutched a few Bibles in my naked arms. I was praying for mercy, praying for courage, praying incoherently.

Suddenly I felt a violent heave and realized I was being pushed toward the train. Soldiers were shouting for us to get dressed. Waves of delirious relief swept over me. I had not been searched! I was sobbing with relief as I flung myself up into the cattle car.

The boxcar had a tiny little window strung with barbed wire at the top of one of the sides. It was difficult to see out of it, but it provided some air. More and more victims were jammed into the car until I thought I would suffocate from the press of bodies— even before we began! There was one jug of water for all of us. I think perhaps there were 100 or 120 men, women, and children in that small car. In one corner was a barrel for our human waste.

The spring days were already beginning to get warm, and everyone was thirsty. We tried to conserve the water, but in no time it was gone. No one was hungry; none wondered about the absence of food. I remember a frail old man beside me who kept repeating that he was 110 years old. One of the village women, Dora, to whom I had witnessed, was in that car with her sister-in-law and their frantic babies. The infants' faces were crimson with the heat and from screaming. Gradually they became exhausted and silent.

After a few hours the waste barrel was full. As the train bumped over rough forest tracks, the contents of the barrel sloshed over onto those having to stand next to it. The stench was almost unbearable. There were tiny nail holes in the sides of the car, and some tried to look out of them or to get air. From the engine we could hear the agonized shriek of the train whistle, as if it gathered our voiceless torment into one repeated cry.

We traveled in that way across Europe for three days and three nights. Once we heard rain beating against the roof of the car. People became desperate. Those near the small high window tried to reach out their hands to catch a drop of rain. One beautiful young girl became insane during the storm and drank her own urine. I tried to comfort the people around me, but my throat was flaming with thirst. I wondered if others thought I, too, was mad as I talked about the love of God. I was as horrified as anyone else.

Finally the train bumped over railroad switches and groaned to a stop. From a nail hole I could see we were at a huge, deserted junction in the middle of nowhere. At first there seemed to be no buildings anywhere in sight. We waited in that fearful state, our clothes stiff and stinking, our tongues swollen with thirst. there was utter stillness. Horror gripped everyone. After a long time, the door was unlocked and flung open, and we were ordered to jump down.

There were Nazi officers, guards, and a group of younger men in odd, special clothes. We didn't know who they were. Later we understood they were Jews called "Capos," prisoners who worked for the SS. We were all so frightened, none of us felt the pain from limbs that had been immobilized for three days and nights. We were in shock from what we had endured. All our little bundles that we had clung to throughout the long journey were instantly thrown to the ground at the order of the officers. The earth was covered with bundles and paper money. People had thrown the money down thinking that their lives might be exchanged for it. Then we ran silently over all that money, driven by the shouts and the rifle butts of the soldiers.

We were ordered to halt before three officers. Later I learned that one of them was the infamous Dr. Mengele, who was in charge of Auschwitz, the camp to which we had come. In all that great mass of humanity there was absolute quiet. No one dared to utter one sound. Even the children were silent.

As we were running along the tracks, the Capos had torn the tiny babies from their mothers' arms and placed them in the arms of the older women. The Capos knew that mothers with babies were rushed straight from the station to the crematoria. The old women also were always sent to be gassed, and in this way the Capos tried to save some of the younger women.

Dora was running beside me. I heard a slight gasp as her beautiful infant was snatched from her arms. It happened so swiftly Dora couldn't even think. She was pushed along with the rest of us, fighting uselessly against the press of the crowd to retrieve her baby.

When we came to a gasping halt before the three officers, all older women (with or without babies) from age forty upward who didn't look strong were sent to the left. Those under forty, healthy, and without children were sent to the right.

113

The three officers wore revolvers in side holsters and carried walking sticks. With a slight lift of the stick, they indicated if a person would go to the left or right. It struck me as unusual that officers should carry walking sticks. Only later I learned that they were actually lethal weapons. The top could be screwed off (as could the bottom) to release a razor-sharp knife which could kill instantly from any angle. The walking sticks flicked the air imperiously, directing people to their fates. Ninety percent were sent to the left.

The officers expressed interest in twins. They had learned the Hungarian word for twins, and they called out *"Ikrek* (Twins)?" when they saw children clinging together who seemed to be the same age. One of the women I knew in the transport had several daughters, and she pushed two forward, thinking she might save them and herself. *"Ikrek!"* she declared. Little did she know that they would be used in the inhuman medical experiments that went on at Auschwitz.

As I lifted my eyes I saw an immense expanse of territory enclosed by a seemingly endless high barbed-wire fence. Watchtowers loomed along the vast margins of the camp. At the top of the nearest, I could see a guard with a machine gun trained intently on us. At other positions, by the gate and along the station platform, were SS men holding the short chains of vicious dogs. Inside the camp were rows of barracks as far as the eye could see.

As soon as the selection was over, we were ordered away in small groups, driven furiously by the Capos' rifle butts that fell on anyone who lagged behind. As we ran blindly forward into the camp, we passed shapeless men and women in striped prison rags, working silently. They only glanced at us. They were so hungry that if a piece of smuggled bread was dropped, they fell on it and began tearing it from one another's hands.

We were assembled in the anteroom of a bath. There an SS woman commanded us to undress in two minutes by her watch, or be killed. Guards fingered their rifles. My shaking fingers found buttons and zippers impossible to manage. Desperately I threw down my precious Bible and began tearing the clothes off my body.

We were driven naked except for our shoes into another room.

Over and over in the days to come I regretted that I had not torn a few pages out of my Bible and hidden them in my shoes. Someone came from behind and grasped my hair. My ears filled with the vicious buzz of a shaver. It seemed no more than an instant before all my body hair was gone, my head as naked as my shamed body.

Next we were lined up for the showers. We were joyful with relief when we saw water trickling from the overhead spigots. By this time some of us knew from the Capos how fortunate we were. After the showers we were given prison rags to wear, and again we were herded outside to form groups of prescribed numbers.

In my group were three sisters, but one of them was suddenly pulled out and ordered to go with a group racing to another part of the camp. The two remaining sisters were horrified at the separation. Guards with their dogs shouted orders at everybody. I knew it was dangerous to make any move, but the anguish of the sisters was very great. I knew no one in my group, and it really didn't matter where I went. I could still see the other group hurrying across the parade grounds. If I were killed for running to the separated sister, I knew only my body would die. I ran for it and miraculously was able to grab the missing sister. "Go back to your sisters," I gasped. "I will stay in this group." (We had already learned that numbers must always be exact.)

In a flash she was gone, and I continued on with the new group to its destination or fate. After awhile, the fear in my heart because of what I had done quieted within me, and to my astonishment I noticed Dora and her sister-in-law running a few paces ahead of me. I was with friends!

We were taken to a huge prison block of 1,500 women and girls. Over the door I saw the German inscription, "Your Block Is Your Home." The sudden green of Piešťany in spring tore into my memory. I was dizzy for a second, shoved along by the press of people behind me. I opened my eyes to see another inscription, "One Louse—Your Death!"

The German officers and SS women and men were afraid of contracting disease from us prisoners. Therefore, they insisted on everyone being clean. But how could one be clean? There was no water. There were many things we still did not know.

Once in the block, we were told to find places in the tiers of wooden shelves that lined the walls, from the cement floor, eight high, all the way to the ceiling. On each level, measuring six and a half to eight feet long, slept nine people, directly on the boards. All these bunks were divided into sections, but there was no curtain or any privacy, so that anyone passing by could see us. We had to sit up or lie down. If we were lying down, we had to be crammed tightly together on our sides so that always I had someone's foot in my mouth or on my head.

At first, thoughts of escaping this unthinkable place raged in my mind. It was inconceivable that I could stay in such a place. There had to be an escape. Actually we had already been introduced to one. It was the high wire fence that encircled the entire camp. "If you wish to run into the wire," one of the officers had shouted when we were still naked and shaking with fear, "such attempts are allowed! People with aspirations discover that the slightest contact with the fence kills instantly! It is forbidden to prevent such people."

The Capos told us we were in Poland in a camp called Auschwitz, Eugene's camp. Nobody knew anything about Auschwitz at the time. It meant nothing of significance to most to learn that we were in this camp, except that my heart cried out for Eugene.

We huddled in the barracks of our block like so many hundreds of stricken monkeys, deprived of everything: of our hair, of our clothes, of our homes, of our people, of our freedom.

I don't know how long it was before we were given water or food. When the food was brought, it was distributed in dirty tin cans, one for each with no spoon or fork with which to eat it. The contents of those cans revolted me. My stomach lurched, and I could not eat. I couldn't eat for weeks. But there were younger women, and some older ones too, who were very hungry and were always eager to get my food.

We were interned in that huge block, sitting or falling back to cover the bodies of others. My arms and legs, used to vigorous exercise and traveling, got terribly stiff and painful. In the morning and in the evening we were taken out of the barracks for the entire camp to be counted.

We learned that there were one million people in Auschwitz. The camp was divided into different sections and lettered "A," "B," "C," etc. The area in which I found myself was Birkenau,

116

the most lethal of all the extermination sections of Auschwitz. In the gas chambers of our camp four million prisoners, mostly Jews, were to lose their lives. It was called Birkenau because of the birch trees. We were in the heart of southern Poland.

For roll call we had to stand in rows, at attention like soldiers on review, one arm's length from the person on each side and one arm's length from the person in front. We stood there for hours in pouring rain, in heat, in cold, each morning and night. Often it rained; we were in the forests, and the cold rain falling on our shorn heads was terrible.

We were a vast, hopeless, motionless sea of misery—thousands and thousands of us, in formation, and woe unto us if one in all that immense multitude was missing! If a prisoner was too ill to stand erectly, if someone slumped or fell over, they were immediately punished. Retribution meant kneeling, sometimes for hours, in piles of broken bricks. Some had their arms lifted up for instant beatings by the SS women who were in charge.

Each of us in Auschwitz received a number. I no longer remember my number—it was so large because there were a million people in Auschwitz. Often the numbers were tattooed on people's arms. That was the fate of the women in the first group in which I found myself. Because I ran to the other group, I became part of a group that was not tattooed. We wore our numbers around our necks.

One of the simplest necessities of life became an unimaginable torment in the camps. The toilet was far away from our block, and permission to use it was extremely difficult to obtain. When we were allowed, the toilets were horrible places of torture, ruled by SS women who were viciously cruel. There were always beatings going on. One had to run, one had to move rapidly. Any distress was met with a rain of blows. There was a spigot there for drinking, but prisoners were pushed through so rapidly that it was a miracle of good fortune to get even a drop of water on the tongue as one raced past.

For the first few weeks I was in such a state of shock that I could not eat. I watched my body deteriorate with a kind of detached objectivity. It didn't seem quite related to me, and it was only after I lost all my body fat and my muscle tissue was beginning to waste away that I was able to force down the watery soup and vile portions of bread.

Gusts of wind raised black dust from the slag gravel that carpeted the camp. Everything was dirty; everything had to be kept clean. Dora grieved constantly for her baby. At times sounds in the barracks resembled a faint dissonant orchestra, tones rising and falling in weeping or praying or complaining as far as the ear could hear. Sometimes sound would die down, only to start up again. Many wept for their husbands and wondered if they were dead or alive. Women longed for their parents, their families, each of their relatives, their homes—all that they had left behind. I was the only one who did not weep at this time. I had already given up all to follow Christ, so I had lost nothing.

It was imperative for everyone to be present at roll call. Anyone staying in the block was instantly taken to the crematoria. Sickness meant death ("work is your salvation"). Sometimes a prisoner would lose the will to live and simply remained in the block, meeting instant death.

Once there was a woman in my block, a formerly wealthy woman, who fell from the eighth level tier and broke her arm. There was no medical attention for such things, and although she was in terrible pain the SS Block Master compelled her to drag herself out for counting. We thought it cruel that she had to stand for hours in terrible pain, but if she had remained behind her broken arm would have sent her to the ovens.

During roll call we could see the huge camp chimneys spewing flames and smoke. Sometimes a SS person would tell us, "Your people are burned here!" Often the Capos would come secretly and whisper these things, but we truly thought they were tormenting us with macabre stories. We couldn't believe that human beings were being burned alive.

One morning my section of the block was called out to go to the "showers." Any change in our severe routine filled everyone with terror. What could it mean? No time to question. Run! Help the injured! Give a hand, someone, to this person or that! Try to stay near the center of the group to avoid the beatings.

The weak and sick formed the edges of our groups, and the rifle butts of the guards fell mercilessly on them. Everyone tried to huddle in the middle of every formation. When we arrived exhausted at the so-called showers, we were ordered to strip. Guards said it was for the purpose of disinfection.

"Remember your numbers," we were assured as we hung our poor dresses on hooks. The undressing was to view our bodies, to judge who among us still had enough flesh to be able to work, who would be liquidated.

"Look smart!" a Capo whispered to me. I immediately drew myself up and tried to appear attentive and healthy. As we were standing there, the dividing of our group took place. It was done silently—most to the left, some to the right. I began again to pray and thank God for His presence.

We were all given a stony piece of gray "soap." Stamped on it were the letters "R.J.F." I remember looking at it curiously, trying to figure out what in the German language the letters might mean. Later I was appalled to learn that the letters stood for "*Reines Juddishes Fett*," which means "Pure Jewish Fat." What I held in my own hands was made from the bodies of Jews after they were gassed.

As I stood staring at the strange soap, I was thrust to the right and pushed into a group leaving the "showers." Another agonizing run across the parade grounds to the block followed, the shouts and curses of the guards following us. There were to be no "showers." The Capos shook their heads at our disappointment. "You have been spared a little longer," they gasped as they ran beside us.

I glimpsed groups of prisoners dragging huge carts full of ashes to the fields. "Those men are scattering the ashes of the Jews as fertilizer over the crops. Others go through the bones and extract gold from the teeth. Others . . ." I ran on, trying to obliterate the hideous tales of the Capos. It was a new kind of torment. The thirst and the marches and the roll calls were not enough.

One Capo who sometimes talked to me entered our block and sought me out. "So you escaped the selection! It is not surprising," he continued. "The ovens are slow. There are too many people for them. Yesterday a whole transport of people arrived. There was no room for them. The camp is packed with people. The new arrivals were taken out to the fields and shot. Then lime was poured over them all."

I think the reason the Capo told me these things was that he

119

saw that I had peace. I knew I was in the center of God's will. I was where He had put me. I did not long for escape or home as others did. I suppose the Capo tried to terrify me into weeping or despair. The prisoners around me in the block knew that I had peace, and sometimes they came to me to talk. Over and over I wished I had just a page of my Bible to share with them. Again I blamed myself for not tearing out a few pages of my Bible to hide in my shoes when we had arrived at the camp!

After the frightening selection at the showers, I was assigned to work. I belonged to Camp B, but I was taken to Camp A, which was a camp of gypsies. Gypsies were persecuted in the same way as Jews. Maybe Hitler thought they originated from the Jewish race. We were all put together in one block and from there were marched to work. Our labor was to carry rain-drenched telephone poles on our shoulders for half a mile. Then we were given saws and ordered to cut the poles into small pieces.

None of us had ever carried heavy burdens before, and we staggered and slid wildly in the mud. I remember how often it rained. We were drenched, and the poles were waterlogged and very heavy. Yet we were thankful to be out of the endless in-activity of the block. We were under God's sky, and although it was forbidden, I was often able to talk to the young girls and women beside whom I labored. I quoted all I could from the Word of God to try and cheer them in some way.

Later we were given different work. We had to bring food to our block in heavy, metal cans. The cans were almost impossible for our weakened bodies to manage, and we were madly dis-tracted by thirst. The rain was our only reprieve. When it stopped, we lived in torment—and not only from thirst.

Absolute cleanliness of the barracks was demanded of all pris-oners, but never were we given a broom, a rag, a drop of water. No mark or spot could be made in the wood, no dirt visible in any corner.

Week blurred into week, but after what I reckoned to be six weeks or two months of labor, there was another sudden shifting of groups and people. Again we were stampeded together into frantic running lines; again we heard the shouting and cursing of the guards, the crack of the rifle butts to the head of anyone unfortunate to run close enough to be reached by an officer. I don't know how all those yellowed bones of sagging skin and panting lungs flung themselves with such speed across the parade grounds and to the shower baths. There was not energy enough for panic. All we heard was the imperative, bursting in the air around us, "Run, pigs! Run, Jewish bitches! Run!"

We were herded into the large anteroom of the showers. "Will they let us wash?" a woman had gasped to me while we were running. I said nothing. I had seen the "showers" once before, and I had not seen water.

An SS officer entered the room and ordered us to strip. Instantly dresses were yanked over poor shaved heads. Swollen, festering welts from the bites of lice and fleas were at once visible, and a forest of bony hands faintly purple hung down lifelessly along the rows of shrunken thighs. There were some children, whose fragile twigs of fingers dug painfully into their mothers' sides. They stared in bewilderment, not at the inspecting SS officer, but at their mothers' vacant faces.

Only a few of us were pulled out of the room. Most remained, pressed forward ever more tightly by the arrival of new lines of people. I could hear a guard shouting, "Nothing painful will happen!" A terrible low moan began, and I saw some people collapsing against the packed bodies around them. The moan rose in a Hebrew chant. Voices filled my head with a pain that grew with the confusion behind me. "*Ani ma'amin be'emuna shlema beviat ha-Mashiah*" (I believe in perfect faith in the coming of the Messiah)." The last words I heard as I hurtled into the blinding light of the pavement was the wail of a child. "Momma! I can't find you!"

No one told those of us who were rejected what to do. Naked, we clustered together outside. We had no orders. We had no clothes. Around the building were lines of guards, uniforms shining with leather and steel. We had no shelter from them save the gray expanse of sky, as naked as we, above our heads. All day we huddled on the pavement at the mercy of the SS. Whatever obscene thing they could imagine to say or do, they did at will. I wondered if we were waiting to be sent back inside. The hours dragged into incoherence. Once I thought I heard Felice say playfully, "You will never be crazy, Rose!" I had forgotten I had a name.

Before roll call an officer suddenly stamped onto the pavement square and ordered us to attention. We scrambled wildly to our feet. We were given a new kind of dress, the same for all of us. It was as gray as the sky and looked like a sack—two pieces of material held together with black buttons. The officer began calling out trades and professions, and we were to indicate if we had any special skills. Certain skills were considered valuable to the SS, and these women were sent away from the rest of us, never to be seen in the camp again.

Finally those of us remaining were ordered to a new block. Many believed that we would be taken out of the camp. There was continuing terror because no one left Auschwitz except to be killed somewhere else.

A day passed, perhaps two. We sat in a frozen torpor, interrupted twice by the nightmare frenzy of the race to roll call. There under the same hopeless sky as before we were counted. In those times I tried to pray, and in a detached and gentle way I was at peace. I felt almost a child, my hand in my Savior's, my wandering thoughts safe with Him.

One morning there was an onrush of guards into our block. An electrifying terror roused us all. "Out immediately! Into lines! Run! Whores! Dogs! Pigs! Dung!" Across the camp we fled in ragged lines, hounded by the snarling, excited dogs, the rushing of the SS around us, the blows to our backs and heads, our exploding lungs. Through the gate and to the freight cars with their doors yawning open to receive us. Again a counting. The number was 1,050, and no one moved until it had been satisfactorily certified. Then up into the freight cars, faster, faster, the mind trying to blank out what might be ahead.

The door heaved shut with a familiar crash. But our situation was quite astonishing to us. We were crowded inside, but not unbearably pressed together. The little air window was not covered over with barbed wire. Our guards were not SS men, but soldiers from the regular German army. To our utter amazement we were even given bread and water. We would have been the desperate envy of every one of the thousands upon thousands we had left behind in Auschwitz. We were to be a slave labor group.

As the train began to slowly pull away from the camp, memories rose in my mind. By the sides of the crematorium I had seen towering masses of women's hair, mountains of phylacteries, heaps of prayer shawls, enough to fill a warehouse, thrown against the buildings, mute witness to the devotion of my people to God. The train wheels couldn't turn fast enough to take me away from the memories that I so desperately wanted to forget. But it is not possible to forget—not even one sight.

We traveled for several days. I think it was a bad journey, but compared to all that we had endured in the camp, it didn't seem terrible. At last the train stopped, and we were ordered to jump out. We had to march through the streets of a city. We didn't know where we were. I was fascinated to see ordinary people left in the world. They stared at us in horror.

Sometimes a townsperson would draw near enough to our lines to ask, "What terrible crimes have you done that you look like this?" They didn't know that our great offense was that we were Jews. They were Germans and by this time had endured almost the entire war, but they knew nothing about the death camps.

We marched at a fast pace for hours. I don't know how long. In the agony I lost track of the time and the day. I was conscious only of my legs rushing along the roads. I felt myself to be floating above the bones and the swollen feet that were beneath me. Some fell and could not get up. Shots rang out throughout the day. Finally we arrived at an anti-aircraft military base. It was situated in the mountains in a little village called Gelsenkirchen. We had traveled from southern Poland, all the way across Germany, almost to the borders of the Netherlands!

In this camp we were placed in three huge tents, 750 people to a tent. Many of us were from Auschwitz, but there were new people as well. The wealthy lady who had fallen and broken her arm in my first block in Auschwitz was there. She was in charge of our tent. I was happy not to have any such position, because places of privilege were given only to those who earned them.

Soon after our arrival, we were taken outside the tents to water faucets. We were delirious with joy. We could drink water! We could wash ourselves! The tap was low and was intended only for drinking, but we rushed under it. The water poured over us, over our gray sacks, our crusted heads. We washed our underwear and put it back on our wet bodies. Everything was done in a terrible rush, because no one knew what would happen next or where we would be taken.

Soon we were packed into the back of huge open trucks. There was a bar across the back of the truck, but too low to protect anyone from falling over the sides. The driver tore along the mountain roads, swerving and lurching on the curving roads. We fell madly against one another, clutching desperately at dresses, bodies, heads, anything to keep from pitching out of the truck and being dashed on the steep cliffs on either side of the road. The ride was to be a daily nightmare.

We arrived at our place of work—an oil refinery that had been demolished by Allied bombs. There was a tiny river near the refinery, running black with wasted oil, which we were to clean of debris.

There were little iron cars on a small railroad track, and bigger cars onto which the contents of the small cars had to be hauled. We were compelled to shove the debris into the cars twelve hours a day. It was excruciatingly hard labor for women and girls in our physical condition. No one dared pause for an instant or the stick of the Capo would come down on one's head. The abuse of the overseers went on all day.

"I'll teach you to work!" Crack! Someone would stagger terribly from a blow. None of us dared look up to see what had happened. "You've never done a day's work in your life! Action! Scum!"

I learned to watch out of the corners of my eyes for the stick of the Capo that might come suddenly down upon me if I did not move quickly enough. At the end of the day we were jammed, utterly exhausted, back into our truck and taken on that fearful ride back to camp. Sometimes at the end of our shift there was shockingly no truck, and we had to march back to the camp.

Long ago my delicate Hungarian shoes had worn out, and I had managed to get a pair of wooden shoes. They were no more than boards tied to my feet with strips of burlap. After a day of heavy labor, marching through the mountains on those shoes was torment. But by God's grace, every night I made it back to camp for food and rest until the next dawn.

One day I was given the job of removing cement from bricks that had been used in the walls of the refinery. We had no tools at

124

all, but the cement had to be cleaned off. It was a blessing of the Lord that I found a sharp piece of iron, and I sat down and began to bang on the brick to get the concrete off. A woman next to me, who had been watching me, finally said, "Tell me, what were you in your former life? You must have been somebody."

The woman was the wife of a rabbi, and she had sleeping space across from me in the tent. I told her all about my life and conversion, and we became friends. She listened as I told her about the Messiah, and when we were back in the tent others drew near to us and I was able to witness.

Among those who listened was a lovely young girl called Ruby, who came from Beregovo, where I had lived. She was so fragile and alone that I became a mother to her and grew to love her very much. Over and over I told her of the love of the Lord Jesus. She was deeply wounded in her mind, but I knew what healing the Lord Jesus could bring to her. We were in that camp for two months, and day after day Ruby listened to me. In a quiet and gentle way she professed Christ as her Messiah, and I saw the grace and peace of the Lord Jesus begin to grow in her.

Just before the end of our stay there, some of the women heard Ruby profess that Jesus was her Lord. They attacked her bitterly. "So now you are a Christian! You are a Gentile! You are like the Nazis who persecute us! Thousands of our people have died, and you turn your back on them. You spit on their memory!"

When Ruby came near these women, they would shove her or spit on the ground as she passed. She grew silent and tried to avoid me. I thought my heart would break to see her turning away from the Lord. With my little strength I prayed that she would remain faithful, but she grew more and more hostile to me and would not speak to me. It was a greater sorrow than the misery of that cold camp and the terrible labor we endured every day. By the time we had to leave the camp, I think she hated me.

But in His mercy the Lord comforted me. One day our labor group was working on coal heaps when a terrible storm came upon us. We fled to some nearby train cars and crawled underneath to protect ourselves from the lightning and the violent downpour. We were all huddled together with no Capo supervision, and for a long time I was able to witness and preach the Word of God. Everyone was terrified of the fury of the storm and of everything that could happen to us alone in those mountains. The women listened intently as I told them the promises of God and how anyone could turn to Him with perfect trust and confidence. It was a wonderful time for me.

Another day I was sent to work inside the ruins of the refineries. Our group was to clear away the debris. We had only our bare hands for moving smashed machinery, heaps of bricks, and sections of walls, pipes, sinks. It was an impossible task. If anyone seemed at a loss as to how to proceed, the foreman screamed at them, "Action! Action!" With bodies that staggered under the lightest weight, we banded together to drag away what we could. I tried to work hard. I told myself again and again that I was doing my labor as unto the Lord.

As I worked I came upon a heavy slab of wood and tried to lift it. To my great joy I discovered some rolls of stiff paper under it! Rapidly I tore off a strip and hid it in my clothing. But that was not the end of my good fortune. In less than a few minutes I also found a few tiny pieces of pencil. At the end of the day I noticed strips of hard plastic lying all around on the ground by the gates of the refinery. This had once been camouflage. I had seen it many times before, but it had meant nothing to me. Now I stopped and snatched up some small pieces, for I had a secret plan. From that day on I began to make a Bible.

It was just a tiny book, but more precious to me than anything I had ever owned. I could now write down Bible verses! I remembered verses from Isaiah 53 and Psalm 22 and wrote them down in my little book. Sometimes I recalled prophecies and verses from the Gospels. As the Lord brought them to my mind, I wrote them in my book.

In our tent were two sisters who knew Hebrew. One of them, Naomi, had managed to steal a little book of Psalms in Hebrew from the great heap of prayer books and other Jewish items outside the crematoria at Auschwitz. I pleaded with her to translate the Hebrew for me. In hurried moments she would read aloud and translate the Word of God. Having a taste of the Scriptures for the first time in so long made me long passionately for a real Bible of my own.

Sometimes our labor took us to the river. By then we knew it was the Ruhr, the site of a massive German industrial center with railway lines connecting its factories and refineries to centers throughout Europe. No wonder it had been heavily bombed, and no wonder it was of the highest priority to make it operative again! From the banks of the river we could hear the Allied shellfire in the distance.

Sometimes German ships would arrive, and we would be marched to the docks to unload the cargo of cast cement blocks for rebuilding the refinery. I had never seen blocks like this because buildings in Hungary are made from bricks or tiles.

We women were compelled to unload these massive blocks. Some of the workers were girls of thirteen or fourteen, some women over fifty. We would haul them off the decks and heave them into the hands of the person next to us in a long chain of workers from the ship to the land carts that would transport them to the refinery. When the job was finally done, we had to wash the ships. We were given buckets and brushes for that.

All this labor was done on one slice of "substitute bread" a day and some hot water with just a few pieces of vegetables floating in it. Once in a very long while they would give us a tiny piece of margarine. It was made from coal, but we thought it a feast!

Some women in our group were pregnant, and they were given a slightly better diet. When it became close to their time, they were transported back to Auschwitz. What was done with their babies no one knew.

Because of the high priority of the work at Gelsenkirchen, there were local German women who worked at the refinery. One day I managed to get close to one of them. I begged her to get me a Bible or New Testament. After a few days this woman smuggled a small German New Testament to me. My hands shook violently as I hid it in my dress. I was unable to speak, to thank her for her kindness.

Over and over as I worked, I slipped my hand inside my dress and felt the substance of the precious little Book. It was not a dream! It was truly there! The hours of the day dragged on. Never had a day seemed so long. I couldn't wait to get back to the tent to share the New Testament with all these women who surrounded me. Many of them spoke German, but they had never read the Bible.

The first person I saw when I returned to the tent was Naomi.

She was frightened by my excitement. "Naomi! I have a New Testament! Now you can have my 'Bible.'" She was elated to have my little homemade Bible with the scribbled verses in it, on which we had worked so long and painstakingly. There were many other verses in it, as well as the sections from the Hebrew Psalms that Naomi had translated for me.

The German soldiers at Gelsenkirchen were much kinder to us than the SS men at Auschwitz. They had been separated from their families for many months, some of them for years. Many didn't know if their wives or parents had survived the terrible bombings of their cities and perhaps, if it were possible, some of us reminded them of the women they had left at home.

When our work was done and we were in our tents in the evening, they left us without abuse, and as long as there was any light at all I was able to read my New Testament and witness to anyone who would listen. I had such joy.

Some women in the tent hated me, especially those from Orthodox Jewish homes. They thought that because I was a Christian I was their enemy, and they did anything possible to vent their bitterness upon me. But the Lord gave me love for them.

One day horror struck us again. Without warning, a small contingent of SS men marched into our camp. Again came the shrill shouted orders, the abuse. Again we were lined up for a selection. This time we were told to strip only to the waist. We stood in the square in front of our tents, the morning wetness of the forest trees dripping on our naked shoulders and heads while the officers marched up and down the rows making the indolent flick of their wrists that indicated who would be sent to the left, who to the right. I remember the beauty of the leaves in their autumn colors, the clouds racing across the windy sky, the world fragrant with the smell of the damp earth and the dying grasses.

Many women ran from one group to another, risking their lives to be with relatives or friends. Many wept, but most stood in the terrible humiliation of the selection, avoiding the merciless eyes of the officers.

My fingers pressed tightly against the New Testament I had hidden in the folds of my skirt. We had to clutch the bottoms of our dresses around our legs, and I wadded the tiny book as deeply into the fabric as I could, fearful that an officer might notice some unnatural position of my hand and suspect I was holding something.

These officers were sent out from Krupp, a strategic steel industry in Essen, an industrial city to the southwest of Gelsenkirchen. We prisoners were to be evacuated because the Americans were concentrating heavily on bombing the refineries in our area, and the Nazis did not want to lose so many hundreds of slave laborers.

Once again I was sent to the right, into the group of women who were to survive and be sent to Essen for labor. Those who remained were shipped immediately by train to the ovens at Auschwitz.

There was no transport for us to Essen, and all the long foot journey we were forced to maintain a rapid pace. Again we ran, jogged, fell forward, gasped for relief, until a kind of unconsciousness set in. To fall to the road meant instant death. Such a prisoner would be trampled by others coming behind, or the butt of an SS rifle would come down on the body for arousal or execution.

We finally arrived at Essen, delirious with fatigue. To our joy, we were ordered into wooden buildings that actually had beds! We rested two to a bed, but our relief at such an unheard of luxury soon changed to desperation. Prior to our arrival, the camp had been occupied by Italian prisoners of war, and the mattresses we were given were full of bedbugs and lice. Soon we were all in agony, and there was no way to get rid of the lice.

In this camp the SS men and women were very nervous and angry, and everyone was beaten regularly. No one escaped the beatings. They were administered for no reason, and it was not possible to avoid them. Here, too, we had to go through two daily roll calls, and from the countings we were taken to the heavy munitions factory at Krupp.

Although none of us had ever operated massive machinery, we were expected to work the machines without any explanation or training. Constantly we were cursed and degraded in every possible way. We were the scum of the earth, vermin, filth underfoot. Never was there anything but cruelty. We would die like animals; we were nothing more than stinking corpses.

I was placed in a large room in that factory where they made huge iron bars. I don't know what they were or for what use they were eventually intended. Each bar was about five or six yards long and had eight sides. Above my head was an electric hammer, and I stood in a little depression in the floor under the hammer. I was told to pull these bars under the hammer and straighten them out.

I tried my hardest to do the work, but often the hammer would come down with too much force and the bar would end up far more crooked than it was to begin with. Often I was terribly beaten for my stupidity. For twelve hours every day I stood in the hole and worked the hammer on the iron bars. Nobody was allowed to talk. If the needs of the body became unbearable and I had to ask to go to the toilet, an SS man would accompany me, his machine gun trained on me as I walked.

In the factory were also some French prisoners of war, but they were strictly forbidden to talk to us Jews. Even so, as they passed by they would whisper, *"Nur langsam! Nur langsam!"* This means, "Only slowly. Only slowly." They meant we should not work efficiently but do as little as possible for the Germans. They were full of courage to dare to speak at all.

But an even worse misery came upon me at that factory—worse than the torment of the lice, worse than the beatings and the cursings of the SS. The anger against me as a Christian grew as our situation became more desperate. The majority of the Jewish prisoners hated me because they said I was a heretic, an enemy of the Jewish people, for I had turned to the religion of the Nazis. I was unspeakably lonely. Over and over I reminded myself that I had the Lord with me, and I claimed the promises of God to His people, Israel. I thought how much He loved them in spite of their treatment of me.

The German women from Essen who worked in the factory had compassion on the young French women who were prisoners of war. Sometimes they smuggled carrots to them or something extra to eat. Occasionally French war prisoners would be allowed to receive packages. They might get a sweater or some food, and such things seemed heavensent to them. It was wonderful to watch them from my hole under the hammer and see happiness for a few moments.

Every morning at 3:30 A.M. we were chased outdoors to be

counted. Many times I would be the last one out because I took a few minutes to lift my heart to the Lord in prayer. This tardiness (although I was not actually late for the call) angered the SS men, and I would be beaten with a whip that had metal knots on the end of leather strips.

To this day I marvel at God's mercy and protection, for my skull was not cracked or my back broken, although I still suffer continually from the aches and pains of those dark morning beatings.

I felt none of us had very long to live; yet I was unable to witness to the hostile Jewish women around me from my New Testament. I felt that if only I had a whole Bible, I could show them from our own Scriptures the prophecies that pointed to Jesus as Messiah. Over and over the women would mock what I said and tell me I was preaching a new religion. They wouldn't listen to the Bible of the Nazis.

I began to beseech the Lord that somehow he would give me a Bible. When I felt I could not bear my existence any longer, and the blackness of night filled my mind, I would call out to the Lord and He would give me encouragement. Time after time He rescued me.

One of the strictest rules at the factory was that Jews were not permitted to speak to any German worker. I wondered at first if I might not risk approaching one of them to beg for a Bible in the same way that I had received the New Testament. But I dreaded another beating from the SS, as I was already ill from the morning whippings. I could not chance discovery.

The guard of our unit was an especially vicious SS woman. One day when I had to approach her for something else, I suddenly blurted out that I wanted a Bible. She stared straight ahead and did not answer me. It seemed a miracle that her shout did not ring out for an SS man to come and beat me. I continued to pray, but I was fearful to try to speak to her again.

Some of the religious Jewish girls kept a devoted count of the days of the Jewish calendar and knew when the High Holy Days were approaching. Soon it would be the Day of Atonement! With almost unbearable intensity I prayed for a Bible, so I could teach from the Scriptures how the Day of Atonement is fulfilled in the Messiah. Over and over I cried out to God for a Bible. Even the din of the factory and the crashing of the hammer on the steel rods, the aching of my body, and the pain in my back from the whippings—all this seemed less real than the anguish of my desire to once again hold a copy of God's Word.

One evening when I was working the night shift, I glanced up and was amazed and frightened to see a familiar SS man standing beside me. Looking straight ahead he whispered an order for me to go to the fence outside the factory the next afternoon at two o'clock. This SS man was the same officer who daily beat me for being the last one at the roll call in the mornings.

Every day in the yard there was a desperate scramble for the lineup. My blockmates would fight each other to get into the line because they were afraid for their lives. The slightest irregularity could mean death or a terrible beating. I didn't bother to push or hurry. I was not afraid to lose my life; I knew I was in God's hands. I was always one of the last because of praying, so I reasoned correctly that it was unlikely that I would ever escape a whipping. This officer cursed me violently and called me every name there was as he whipped me. Now he was telling me to go to the fence.

In an instant he was gone. At the morning roll call I prayed that I would live until two o'clock. It was the day before the Day of Atonement. I was too excited to sleep, and when the time drew near I dragged myself from the lice-infested mattress and made my way to the fence. I was shaking with anxiety and expectation. Perhaps I would be killed.

Waiting on the other side of the fence was the SS officer himself. I drew near to him, trembling with excitement. I could tell nothing from his face, but something in his eyes flickered as he thrust a little book, wrapped in white tissue paper, through the fence. "You will have to hide this," he said as he hurried away.

The Lord had performed a miracle in that terrible place and had incredibly used my vicious enemy to give me a Bible! I rushed dizzily back to the barracks, knowing I held in my hands a proof of God's love and grace. He had not forsaken me! He had given me the desire of my heart!

The sun set. It was the Day of Atonement. Many of the women in the barracks spoke only Yiddish. Eagerly I translated the precious book for those who didn't understand German. It was electrifying to everyone that I had received such a gift for the Day of Atonement. Many listened!

It was hard for the women to believe that the same officer who whipped me would give me this Bible. Later it was discovered, through an SS woman, that his first wife had been a Jewess. Perhaps because of her, he took pity on me.

We didn't know that the war was drawing to a desperate close. We knew the bombings on Essen were merciless. The city itself was so razed by bombs that there was no transportation. We had to walk the five miles from the camp to the factory every day. My makeshift wooden shoes continued to make the marches intensely painful. By this time the burlap strips that tied them to my feet had disintegrated, and I used bits of string instead which wore through my skin and rubbed into the bones.

Our hair had not grown back, and only folds of skin hung on our bones. Because of the bombings of the city, all the water mains were broken. Consequently, for a time there was no water as well as no food, and our thirst became unbearable.

Once I pulled my skin away from my body and noticed that it stretched a foot or more from my bones. Like everyone else, I was tormented by hunger and thirst. But I had my Bible!

I found a little piece of material and borrowed a precious needle from one of the women. By pulling some thread from the material of the gray sack I was still wearing, I was able to sew a little purse for the Bible, which I then hung around my neck under my dress. Since I had lost so much weight, it didn't show at all, and I was able to keep the Bible safe with me at all times.

The women prisoners were terrified of the bombings which fell near us day after day. Now I had the Scriptures to comfort them. They didn't have to believe only what I said—I had proof from God's Word! I could show them the way of salvation and hope through the prophecies. With a weak voice and cracked lips, I read to them the wonderful promises of God which showed He would not make an end of the nation of Israel. There was not much time for this kind of witness, except when the bombs were raining down upon us and we were huddled in a corner of a shelter.

We were all getting weaker and weaker. It was already the

133

beginning of October, and it seemed very cold. There was almost no food. Twice a day we got a small portion of soup. Sometimes there was a piece of turnip in it or a piece of meat. The meat was so rotten it sickened us, but we were ravenous and ate it anyway. Other days a blackened, rotten onion would be thrown into the soup.

Our bread was very hard and mixed with sawdust. When I first saw this bread at Auschwitz I thought it was a piece of wood or brick and used it for a pillow under my head—until it was stolen!

For a long time I had tithed my food. Mr. Miller had taught me to tithe, and since I had no money I had tried to give away a tenth of my food. The Lord gave me mercy for this. But in those terrible days I did not tithe. It was not only the lack of food and water and the labor that debilitated us. When we returned from the night shift, we could not rest. We had to share our beds, and there was so much quarreling and turmoil and noise that it was impossible to sleep. Our existence was a living death.

One day in October as I was working at my machine, I collapsed. The last thing I saw was the emotionless face of the very strict SS woman who supervised my area of the factory. I thought I would be instantly killed, but she helped me to a bench. Many hours passed, and I just lay there on that bench. When the shift was over, I was pulled to my feet and made to march the five miles back to camp. Some of the women in my barracks held my arms and helped me walk every step of that agonizing journey.

In the camp I was told to report to the "hospital." It was just another cell block with a woman in a white coat who pretended to be a doctor. I think her husband had been a doctor, but she wasn't even a nurse. There was no medicine—absolutely nothing at all—but I was permitted to lie on a mattress. I was completely paralyzed; I could not move my limbs or speak.

The bombing of the city intensified every day, and SS and prisoners alike were petrified of the bombs. We had no real protection. Our shelters were holes dug in the ground, covered with a thin roof of concrete about the thickness of a woman's hand. There wasn't even a door to the bunkers.

In the hospital when the air raid siren sounded, everyone would run out and leave me and a paralyzed girl alone in the building, along with this young girl's sister who stayed with her.

So the three of us would be together, and I could pray and witness to them. I was very tired and so weak that I could barely force myself to speak. I confess that while I prayed for the safety of the two terrified girls, I was asking for God's mercy to let me die. I thought I couldn't bear more! Because I was so ill and because the bombs were almost always direct hits, I was sure the Lord would take me one way or another, and I was very thankful.

One day I opened my precious Bible, and the Lord gave me the message that I would live. I read 2 Corinthians 1:8-10, where Paul writes of his own troubles:

> For we do not want you to be unaware, brethren, of our affliction which came to us in Asia, that we were burdened excessively, beyond our strength, so that we despaired even of life; indeed, we had the sentence of death within ourselves in order that we should not trust in ourselves, but in God who raises the dead; who delivered us from so great a peril of death, and will deliver us, He on whom we have set our hope. And He will yet deliver us.

From the moment of reading those verses, I knew that God wanted me alive. Even though I was bitterly disappointed, I was glad to know His will and to be spared the state of indecision.

I had been witnessing to the "doctor" and shared with her portions of the Bible. I even felt that she was a little friendly toward me. But one day she came to my bed and announced, "You will have to get out. You must go back to your barracks and return to work!"

I was aghast! I couldn't even stand up for a second. How could I go back to my barracks? How could I return to work?

But, of course, there was never any argument with anyone who gave orders, no matter who he was. That would be a sure way to bring beatings and worse trouble. The sister of the paralyzed girl lifted me up, and together we staggered back to my barracks. She supported my weight, which by that time was not very much.

That night there was a terrible bombing attack on our camp for the first time. Until then, the bombs had fallen on the city of Essen itself, but now the town was completely demolished. The Krupp factory was on the outskirts, and it had not been hit. But now our factory and camp were the targets.

The Allied bombs were made of phosphorous. These bombs

not only explode, but anything the bomb fragments touch immediately bursts into flames. In those days dense, white phosphorous clouds hung continuously over Essen, mixed with the blackened spirals from miles of smoking rubble. We had seen the raging fires from these bombs, but now the bombs began to rain on our camp.

When the order to take shelter came, everyone fled in absolute hysteria from the barracks into the bunkers. I was so weak I was unable to move, so I just stayed on my bed and waited for the bombs. The barracks were made of thin wood. I was in a tinder-box.

I began to reflect on the thought that I had deliberately disobeyed the order to seek shelter. Perhaps fear would have propelled me to the shelter if I had tried, or perhaps the Lord would have miraculously helped me. But I had simply stayed in my bed. Suddenly the thought came to me that I was really committing suicide. How would I face the Lord? I would come into His presence because of my own disobedience. He had told me He had a purpose for me to live, and I had rebelliously chosen to stay behind in the barracks and be blown up!

Often I was actually happy when the Allied bombs came, but now I was in agony. I could hear them hissing as they exploded, and I could feel the heat from the fire and taste the acrid phosphorous in the smoke. One end of the barracks was already in flames. There was a whooshing as the sheets of fire devoured the dry wood.

I begged the Lord to forgive my disobedience. I promised Him if He kept me alive this time, I would not willfully stay out of the shelters again. Gradually the terrible noise of the planes and the bombing lessened. With all my strength I dragged myself to the door of the next room. All the ceiling beams had crashed to the floor and the room, and every other room in the barracks, had been destroyed by the fire. God in His mercy had spared that one area in which I was praying.

By our kitchen barracks there was a storage place where potatoes and huge beets were kept. Some of the starving women stole beets. This was considered to be a most heinous crime and was reported to the head of the camp, called the Lagerführer. He was the one to punish such a crime. And he knew no mercy.

One day the entire camp was ordered out for roll call and a search. Every human body had to be examined for stolen food. I had my Bible hidden on my body in the little bag hung around my neck. It was punishable by death to have any possession or anything hidden, but I could not give up my Bible. I felt I had to have it to survive. I felt I had been through so much already—hunger, thirst, filth, labor, bombings, beatings, abuse—that I could not endure life without God's Word.

When my turn came, I had to pass by the Lagerführer and the other officers for the search. It took them only an instant to discover my Bible. The Lagerführer ripped it off and struck me to the ground. "You should work and not read your Bible," he screamed. Yet he did not shoot me as he would have if I had had food.

I tried to get up on my feet, but he continued to beat me, yelling again and again, "You are to work, not read!" I was horrified. I could not find my Bible in the dirt. After a few moments I could see only his stick crashing down on my bones. I was too weak to struggle. My mouth was filled with dirt, and I forgot why I was being beaten. I could think only of my Bible.

"Please, Herr Lagerführer, sir, the Herr of the camp," I gasped, "please . . . my Bible." I remembered to ask nicely. Mother taught us to ask courteously . . . Mother and her prayer book by the riverbank . . . the sunlight glinting on its silver cover . . . my little Bible.

"Please, Herr Lagerführer . . . sir . . ."

An officer dragged me to my feet. I fell into the unmoving line of women prisoners yet to be searched. I couldn't remember what had happened, only that somehow I had lost my Bible. The officer threw me out of the line, toward the barracks. Perhaps someone helped me, I don't know. My Bible was gone. There was nothing I could do.

The bombings of our camp grew worse each day. It was a huge camp and actually belonged to Buchenwald, which is why the SS controlled it and why conditions were so severe. The Allied planes dropped tons of phosphorous bombs on the camp. Night after night came the explosions of fearful white light, dazzling and igniting. Water cannot extinguish phosphorous fires—they have to burn out by destroying everything that can be burned, and if a prisoner caught a bit of gel from the bomb on his skin, terrible burns resulted.

In the raids, I was always the last one to come into the bunkers and thus was nearest the door. There was much weeping and screaming in those packed bunkers, and I cried out to the Lord for mercy for all the prisoners because I knew they were unsaved and only seconds away from eternal death. Over the hissing of the bombs I shouted the words of the prophet Habakkuk:

> *Art Thou not from everlasting, O Lord, my God, my Holy One? We will not die. Thou, O Lord, hast appointed them to judge; and Thou, O Rock, hast established them to correct. Thine eyes are too pure to approve evil, and Thou canst not look on wickedness with favor. Why dost Thou look with favor on those who deal treacherously? Why art Thou silent when the wicked swallowed up those more righteous than they?*

The terror of the women subsided, and they hung on every word I said for any shred of hope that they might survive the horror of the bombings.

One night after the bombing we staggered out of our bunker to a dreadful sight. All the buildings of our camp were blackened shells, pouring smoke. Some buildings were still blazing. The sky was orange. We stood shocked. In that hot light I suddenly saw the Lagerführer standing with a twisted look on his face. I think he knew then that it was all over, and he didn't know what to do.

I had been praying for him ever since the beating he gave me. He was one of the most wicked of all the SS men I had known. Suddenly the Lord gave me boldness, and I stepped around some little fires and made my way to where he was standing staring at the camp. He seemed not to notice me, and when I addressed him he gazed at me vacantly.

"Herr Lagerführer, sir, leader of the camp, please may I have my Bible? I have been praying for you. Will you please give me back my Bible now?"

His eyes moved away from me and surveyed the vast destruction spread out in all directions. I waited, hardly daring to breathe. Finally after a long time he answered absently, "*Schon gut! Schon gut! Sie können's schon haben!* (All right! All right! You shall have it!)." And then, dreamlike, he moved away.

It was God's mercy that all human life did not perish in the bombing that destroyed our camp. But now we prisoners had nothing at all—no blankets, no places to lie down, no food, no reason to exist because the factory had been destroyed. We ought to have been immediately transported to Buchenwald itself for execution, but the ovens were utterly unable to keep up with the exterminations and so we were spared.

All of us wondered what would become of us. Even the SS were worried about their own fates. One day I saw the Lagerführer again and confronted him, pleading for my Bible.

He was occupying a corner of a barracks that remained, and he told me to come to his quarters at a certain time. I was torn with anxiety. I had a shred of hope that my Bible had somehow survived the fires and that he meant to give it back to me; yet I greatly feared what torment he might devise to do to me. The other women speculated vividly what would happen to me when I went to his barracks. But I was determined to try to regain my Bible.

As I made my way to his barracks, I could feel the eyes of groups of women on my back. I picked my way unsteadily through the nightmare of rubble to where the Lagerführer lived.

In spite of the filth of the camp, the Lagerführer was immaculately dressed. I was astonished at how his boots shone in the charred ruins at his doorstep. When I arrived, he immediately handed me the Bible. It had been taken to the wooden shack near the entrance to the camp where we had to line up twice a day for counting. The shack had burned to the ground, but the Bible had not even been singed! He looked at me strangely. "I shall not see you reading this book!" he warned.

But he had not said, "You are not allowed . . . !" In a lurching, hobbling haste of swollen feet and cracked bones, I ran to my companions. We all were astonished that he had returned the Bible and also that it had not been burned.

I began to read the book of Isaiah, and every word was wonderful to me. My soul fed on this book constantly. I remember rejoicing and weeping over chapter 33:

> *The Lord is exalted, for He dwells on high; He has filled Zion with justice and righteousness. And He shall be the stability of your times, a wealth of salvation, wisdom, and knowledge. The fear of the Lord is his treasure.*

I was able to share much of Isaiah with my fellow prisoners because they knew it was the book of Judaism, not the Christian books of the New Testament. How wonderful were the words

> *Your eyes will see the King in His beauty; They will behold a far-distant land. Your heart will meditate on terror. . . . Your eyes shall see Jerusalem an undisturbed habitation. . . . But there the majestic One, the Lord, shall be for us a place of rivers and wide canals, on which no boat with oars shall go, and on which no mighty ship shall pass— . . . And no resident will say, 'I am sick'; The people who dwell there will be forgiven their iniquity.*

When our hunger and thirst would become almost unbearable, I would read Isaiah 33:16 over and over:

> *Such as these shall dwell on high. The rocks of the mountains will be their fortress of safety; food will be supplied to them and they will have all the water they need.*

The Lord Jesus was my Bread, the Living Bread, and He was the Living Water, too.

The women around me saw how much I loved the Bible, and that I had been willing to risk my life for it. In earlier days, when we were in the bomb shelters, they would ask me to tell them again and again about the promise that God would not completely destroy Israel; but when the bombing was over, they mocked me again.

Now they began to take the Bible very seriously and asked me, "Rose, what does it say is going to happen?" There was so much encouragement I could give them. In Deuteronomy are the words: "You [Israel] will seek the Lord your God, and you will find Him if you search for Him with all your heart and all your soul."

The women were comforted as I repeatedly told them that the Bible promised, "Thus says the Lord, Who gives the sun for light by day, and the fixed order of the moon and stars for light by night . . . 'If the heavens above can be measured, and the foundations of the earth searched out below, then [and only then] I will also cast off all the offspring of Israel for all that they have done,' declares the Lord."

But daily existence grew worse and worse. The SS had to think of something to do with the 550 of us who had survived. The city of Essen was a total ruin. Not a single inhabitable building stood. The factory had been demolished, and the streets from the factory to the town were impassable. The SS found a cellar in a building in Essen, and they forced all 550 of us into it to be confined. We were, after all, still under arrest as Jews. There was nothing in the cellar—no washrooms, no dividers, no beds—absolutely nothing. Yet in this way, the SS continued to obey their orders.

In that cellar, people found what they could—perhaps a board to lie down on, or a rag for a pillow. Everyone fought and stole from each other, and again I became an enemy to my companions. They no longer feared that they would be killed. I was a Christian outcast.

I found a wooden box in a corner of the cellar and made it my bed. Winter was already approaching, and the air outside was cold. The walls of the small cellar began to drip with moisture from the heat of so many bodies jammed together.

There was one tap in the cellar for the 550 of us. We were dreadfully thirsty and filthy besides. In that cellar we were given half-rations: a small amount of soup with a tiny fragment of turnip in it once a day, along with a single slice of "bread."

There was a sewer in the cellar that we had to use for a toilet. Soon it was blocked, and the sewer backed up and ran over onto the floor until the foulness reached six inches deep. Splashing into it was the water that condensed from the ceiling and fell down onto us.

It was unspeakably horrible, and we were deliriously thankful to be taken out of this confinement every day for work. The SS never gave up, but continued with their orders that we were to work until we died. Although the city was totally demolished, we were to ignore the decaying bodies in the streets, and work!

Our job assignment was at a factory ruins miles from the cellar. Wet and foul as we were, we had to walk in the freezing air to the site. At first we had to carry debris from one place to another—heavy pieces of iron and metal sheets which were sharp and crazily twisted from the bombs. The SS were always around us, with guns in our backs if anyone paused or faltered in the work.

We were given pickaxes and had to dig. None of us had even lifted a pickax before. We staggered under the weight, but we had to dig or hear the click of the safety catch released on the rifles behind us. It was now bitter cold, and I had still the wooden shoes on my feet, but no stockings. I wondered if my legs would actually freeze. They were deathly blue and painful. I feared they might be frozen already, but reminded myself that they were causing too much pain to be frozen.

One day I was amazed when a German townsman suddenly drew near me in the ruins and laid a pair of heavy stockings in front of me and left. Perhaps he had asked his wife for them. I snatched them up and pulled them on in frantic haste. Fortunately the attention of the SS was not on me at the moment. This was a great mercy of the Lord.

But an even greater mercy was yet to come!

Snow was beginning to fall on the city, and it became intolerable for me to walk on the boards that had served me so long as shoes. In our work detail were not only Jews, but also French and Dutch prisoners of war. They were always kept strictly away from us in separate camps and were given more food and clothing, because it was not deliberately intended that they should die. It was very dangerous for them to have any contact with us but on rare occasions, before our camp and factory were demolished, a Frenchman or Dutchman would give food or help a Jew if he could.

One day I was struggling in the snow with my ax, slipping and falling to my knees because my feet were frozen on the wooden boards, making me stumble. I was thinking of the poor Hungarian soldiers I had seen at the beginning of the war, whose feet and fingers and ears had been frozen and were festering. I was dreaming of the biscuits I had baked and taken to them, when suddenly a French prisoner rushed over to me and threw a huge pair of men's shoes in front of me. I didn't have time even to look up to see him or thank him.

My stiff fingers tore off the strings that held the boards on my feet. It was wonderful to put my feet inside those men's shoes. I wept at the mercy of God and the human kindness of the French prisoner.

Even though there was nothing left that I could see of Essen, bombings continued all through December 1944. It was a bitterly cold winter in Germany, and as we prisoners moved half dead through the motions of our labors, the SS soldiers and women overseers built fires in the snow and warmed themselves, cursing at us for our ineffective efforts.

One day as we were marching to our work site, our line edged just a little closer to the SS fire so that we could feel an instant of warmth as we passed by. It seemed no one noticed. But that night when we arrived back at our wretched cellar, there stood one of our own Jewish women with a whip, which she cracked furiously over her head.

"You tried to warm yourselves at the fire!" she screamed, wildly beating us. "You didn't do any work, and you won't get any food!" The whip cut into our bodies, but more painful was the fact that she was one of our own. It was horrifying enough in our conditions to be whipped by the SS, but when a Jew did it, it was far more dreadful. And so our suffering grew worse and worse as the time of Christmas grew closer.

I wondered if we would be allowed to rest on Christmas Day. It was a holiday for all German people and the prisoners of war. But as a punishment (for what, we didn't know), on Christmas morning we were chased out of our cellar to work in the snow. We were given the task of carrying debris from one place and heaping it in another. It was just a useless task to make us work. But in the afternoon, we were left alone. Many of us ate snow to have something in our stomachs and to quench our thirst.

Some of the women had managed to get some matches, perhaps from the French, and they built a fire. We filled buckets with snow and melted it, and then in that biting cold we took off our clothes and washed them. There was nothing to do but put them back on again wet, but we thought it was a wonderful day because we could wash, even without soap! I was cursed by the women and pushed aside until the others were finished with the water. It was a Nazi holiday, and a Christian one, to the women. But in spite of their anger, it was glorious to be able to wash!

From time to time new transports of prisoners would be brought to Essen. They were housed in the remains of the burned barracks, although we Jews were kept packed in the cellar, fouled by the sewer and our close confinement.

One day when all the work details were out digging, there was a daytime bombing and all of us, Jews and Gentiles alike, had to run together to find shelter. Some new prisoners were Russian women brought into Germany when German forces were retreating from Russia. They were sentenced to hard labor, but their work was much easier than ours. Because I knew Russian, I began talking to one of the women as we huddled together during the bombing. Immediately I found out she was a born-again believer!

The frozen earth under our feet was heaving from the bombs. All were covering their heads and weeping. Smoke and flames and the terrifying hissing swirled around us, but this woman and I clung together, laughing and praising the Lord in our joy at having found each other. After so many months of hatred from my companions and beatings and contempt of the SS, it was heaven to see this woman's smile and feel her arms around me.

From that day on, whenever she could, she gave me an extra onion or a bit of other food as a token of love. I never wept from the beatings or the bombs, but her face was so dear to me that just to see her in the distance would bring tears to my eyes. She was soon caught giving me food and removed from the camp. I never saw her again.

The January cold in the grip of winter in our cellar became intense. I began to wonder if I would freeze to death. The others kept alive at night by huddling together, but no one would let me come near them. Sometimes I shook so badly from the cold I would rattle against the side of my box, and the others would scream and curse me for making a disturbance. I prayed constantly that the Lord would help me endure.

One of the women in the cellar decided to try to clean away some of the frozen refuse from the floor. I watched her from my box, unable to move my bones from the cold. As I stared, marveling that she had the strength to move about in such cold (although she had a coat), I saw she was cleaning the floor with a piece of sheepskin. There was a little commotion on one side of the room. Some of the other women were handling something and then threw it into a corner in disgust. I saw that it was a man's fur coat, like the Russians wore. It was just simple sheepskin, very rough and fur-lined. With all my heart I longed to have that coat. The woman cleaning the floor had torn a sleeve out of it and was using it as a broom.

I was afraid to let my companions know that I wanted the coat. I was sure they would tear it up rather than let me have it. They didn't want it for themselves because they were afraid that it was full of lice. I was so desperately cold I didn't care. Besides, we all had lice anyway, and I thought a few more couldn't make one any sicker or more uncomfortable.

After a while, I made my painful way to the coat and grabbed it. As fearful as a thief I hurried back to my box. In our group was a woman who was so unpleasant and who constantly used such foul language that nobody wanted her either. When she saw what I had done, she came to me and we huddled together under that coat. We didn't take any of our clothes off, not even our shoes, it was so cold.

Since I didn't have permission from the SS to wear the coat, in the morning at roll call I approached the Lagerführer and asked permission to wear it. The winter storms were at their worst, and he granted me my request. I found a torn piece of blanket and from it fashioned a sleeve to complete my fur coat.

That coat saved my life, but it caused the other prisoners to hate me all the more. To my delight, I discovered that it had been treated so that lice could not survive in its fur. Not only was it protection from the cold, but also from lice!

I wore the coat day and night, and the women were consumed with jealousy. They didn't want to hear how the Lord had answered my prayer and spared my life by means of the coat. They pretended to believe it was full of lice, and whenever I came near they screamed, "Get away from us! You are crawling with lice! You are lousy! Get away!"

The coat had belonged to a huge man, and although it was only a jacket, it came well below my knees. I was nothing but skin and bones, and my legs stuck out of the coat and into those huge men's shoes that the Frenchman had given me. The SS officer that marched with us to work used to shout at me, "Old goat! Faster! Faster!" I was then thirty-five and still had no hair on my head, but he called me only an old goat. I was fortunate that he had such a nice name for me.

Life itself seemed utterly useless. All day we lifted and carried debris and made piles of it in the snow. We moved like people in a trance, stirred only slightly by the shouting of "Action!

Action!" by the SS. Then evening would come, and we would stumble back to the filthy cellar, the bitter quarreling, and the biting of the cold and the lice.

I clung to the assurance that I was in the place where the Lord had put me. Everything was permitted by Him, and I knew that when the bombs would start to fall, the women would stop cursing me and pushing me away. Then they huddled around me; they saw that I had peace in spite of the bombings and thought that somehow I would be safe. In those times I could talk to them about the Lord, and they would listen and ask me to pray. I often read the books of Jeremiah and Ezekiel. I knew I was to be a witness whether the desperate people to whom I was sent listened or not. I was to speak. The Lord had told me to warn them, and if they would listen they would be saved. If they would not listen, I knew the Lord would not blame me.

In that last bitter winter of the war, time seemed to have stopped. Death did not deliver us; yet we breathed, ate, and lay down in its corruption.

One morning in March as we were lined up for the counting in the winter dark, I could see that the SS men and women were extremely nervous. We were ordered into numerical units and told to sit in the snow and wait for further orders. I tried to fold my bones inside my sheepskin coat. Others suffered more. Finally we were told to get up and march. We were frightened because we were each given a whole loaf of bread. What could this mean? We knew that something was going to happen.

We stumbled along the bombed roads for hours. I could tell from the signs that we were proceeding southwest toward Düsseldorf. Everywhere was devastation, and although we had never been given news of the war, I could see that Germany was in ruins. Eventually I could no longer focus my vision. I entered a delirium—my legs moved, my ears registered the cursings of the SS, my back felt the jabbing of the SS rifle barrels, but my mind floated above my body, observing the progress of an old goat in human facsimile, staggering along a landscape charred and desolate and dreamlike in its absence of reality.

At some railroad tracks we were suddenly ordered to halt. Everyone collapsed instantly. The rifles rained down blows like hailstones, and soon we were on our feet again, obeying the command to climb into the fearful transport cars, their sides gaping open to receive us. But there were not so many of us for each car this time—perhaps fifty girls and women to a car. Strangely, even the SS came aboard with us, although they had always had their own coaches, not cattle cars like ours. We traveled uneasily for many days, stopping at stations along the way, when the doors would be heaved open for air and light, and for the SS to exercise. It would not have been difficult to try to run away, but I was not willing. I knew God wanted me to be where I was.

When the women were rested, they began to curse me again and made life as unpleasant for me in the cattle car as they had in the cellar. But I understood more clearly the purpose for my being with them. Sometimes there would be a bombing attack and the train would stop. The engineer and the SS people would jump off and flee for shelter, but we were left locked in the cars while the bombs fell.

Then the women would plead to hear about God's forgiveness and His salvation. Again and again I would tell about the Messiah who was willing to die on the cross for my sins and theirs. I assured them of God's promises to our people. For the first time I began to remember that God had a plan to regather our people into Palestine, and I gladly told them that. There would be a new country.

They simply couldn't understand it. They said that if they were ever free, they would return to their homes, to their cities and villages, find their relatives, and start life all over. It would be as it was. In spite of what our eyes told us, we couldn't believe we no longer had homes or villages or relatives to go back to!

The train journey was very long, and we had no water. I had a little salt, and I shared it with my companions. We licked a few grains every day and made our loaves of bread last as long as we could. The train started and stopped many times. There were long, countless waits. Later I found out that our destination was to have been Buchenwald for extermination, but for some reason it was not possible for the train to go there. Eventually we made a final stop. The doors of the boxcars were dragged open one last time, and we were ordered to jump out and form marching positions again.

The SS men were furious at the necessity for another march. We were commanded to run or die. As we rushed crazily over the blackened countryside, they kept hitting us with their guns and pushing us faster and faster. We were terrified at their anger. No one could guess where we were going. Gradually we saw the outline of an enormous camp in the distance. When we got closer, my heart leaped to see Hungarian soldiers. But they were stern, guarding the camp with fierce faces. I felt desperately betrayed.

We were shocked to see thousands and thousands of people in the camp. There were wooden barracks, consisting of one room each, stretching miles to the horizon. All 550 of us from Essen were put into one room! Already in the room were French prisoners of war, many of them elderly women. Previously, any foreign prisoners of war had always been kind to Jews, but these women hated us. Perhaps it was the terrible crowding. We took up so much precious space. I spoke some French because of the lessons Mademoiselle had given me at Piešťany. Because I could speak a little, they were decent to me. But in this new place death so pervaded the camp that people who had any energy lived in hate, and would gladly have killed for a piece of bread.

Here in Bergen-Belsen there was no bread. There was no food at all for the thousands and thousands of dying prisoners who were heaped into the barracks like refuse. Once a day half a cup of black liquid called "coffee" was given to each of us. It was a kind of burned wood, perhaps even oak.

I remembered Auschwitz in the beginning when I could not eat for weeks because the food was vile. Now at the last I searched with aching eyes for anything on the ground that I could devour. If I found a bit of raw potato peeling, I snatched it up as if I had found a fortune. Perhaps I might come across a fragment of rotten garbage that some SS worker had thrown away. Even my eyes were hungry.

The work we had to do at this camp was to dig mass graves. I was still considered strong enough to hold a shovel and push away the earth. Other women in macabre teams had to drag the corpses into huge tents. Hundreds and thousands, all unburied. The SS were frenzied. They wanted all those corpses buried, because they knew that soon the camp would be liberated. They wanted what they had done covered and out of sight. Girls pulled the corpses, stiff and green and blue, into the shallow ditches I dug. Hour after hour, day after day our grisly work dragged on. To stop meant immediate death.

Sometimes prisoners would manage to steal a bite of raw vegetable—perhaps when they were picking up the SS garbage cans. When they were caught, they were forced to hold the food in their mouths while they knelt to be shot above the mass graves. If there were bullets to spare, they would be shot. If not, they would be pushed alive into the graves and covered over. We had to keep on with our work, the guns of the SS in our backs and the cursings and the shoutings of "Action! Faster!" in our ears.

The poor dead! I threw the earth on top. I dug. I moved. Sometimes I crawled because I could not walk. One day I began to eat grass like some of the others. An SS woman saw me and slapped my face. It meant nothing. I only groped for my shovel. But it was a moment of importance even though I did not know it. It was the last time in my life I was ever to be hit by a Nazi!

By now hundreds were dead in our own barracks, but there was no one with the strength to move them. We simply sat among them or lay beside them when we were allowed to stop working. Soon enough the shouting and cursing of the SS would begin again, and we would be forced out to the graves and to our work. All of us were sick, consumed by thirst, many hopelessly dying from dysentery.

One morning there was no shouting of the SS. The hour for work came and there was silence. After a time a few people cautiously dragged themselves out of the barracks. Then more. It was April 14. There was a shout from somewhere that all the guards had fled! Prisoners stumbled into the streets of the camp. The watchtowers were empty. I saw some Hungarian soldiers running out of the front gate of the camp; then there was no one left. Only prisoners.

Pandemonium broke out. Hundreds still strong enough smashed into the kitchens and started pulling out everything there was. Thousands of the people still alive in that camp had been prisoners and slaves for years. Now they found themselves without guards! There was nobody standing ready to shoot them down or beat them. People went mad.

Everyone grabbed anything possible: raw potatoes, dry crackers, dry bread, underwear, outer clothing. Everything in the storehouses was thrown into the yard. Everyone snatched something—it didn't matter what—just to have a change of clothes, just to tear off the filthy infested rags. Even I got something to put on.

I stumbled out of the mass of struggling bodies. The delirium that had energized me drained away, and I wanted water desperately. All was confusion. In the distance I saw a friend. It wasn't surprising. Everything was a dream, and I staggered toward a figure that stood in the multitude and looked back at me. It was Mary, the little girl whose father had been a millionaire and who came to Piešťany every summer. Mary's Christian father had given me the little Scripture book that I had once loved as a child. Now Mary was a grown skeleton and was watching me make my way toward her. What was she doing in the camp?

When I came close I almost passed her. I could think only of somehow finding some water. Mary's eyes were rimmed with tears. She, too, had found something to cover herself with and was no longer clothed in the rags of the camp.

"Rose?" she called weakly. I stared at her. "Rose!" Her arms went around me, and we fell together to the ground. She too was in Bergen-Belsen! She was not a dream! I touched her papery face and her arms. We wept and rejoiced, but I could see she was as ill as I.

She had found in the camp a doctor her father had once known. The doctor had been able to give her some medicine. He also had told her secretly where there was one water faucet still working.

We found cups, and supporting each other we tried to find the water tap. The sounds of fighting led us to it. Hundreds of people were desperate for even a drop of its water. There was an inexplicably huge Ukrainian woman beside me and when she saw me struggling to get some water, she slapped me in the face. "Get away from me, you Christkiller!" As I collapsed, in that instant, over the loudspeaker in clear English came the announcement that we were liberated. Then the message was repeated in German and in all the other languages of the camp.

The noise of the loudspeakers was bursting in my ears, and prisoners were shouting and stumbling in every direction. I was still on the earth and I wept. I had not been able to get a drop of water.

VII

Deliverance

MY FIRST MEMORY of liberation was the sight of
British trucks rolling into the camp, bearing
huge tanks of water. They gave everybody
water, as much as was wanted. Whoever could
walk got it first, and buckets to carry away with them.
Then the soldiers rushed into the barracks with water for
those unable to come out.

It was a time of horror for the soldiers. Many told later that the
army could smell the stench of the camp eight miles away as they
made their approach on the road. Every man of them was filled
with dread as they entered Bergen-Belsen, but none was prepared
for the hideous panorama of tens of thousands of unburied corpses
that rose up before their eyes. Many wept and stood stunned. All
were appalled. Even the officers didn't know what to do.

After the water, they brought in barrels of powdered milk. We
Europeans knew sweet milk and canned milk but had never seen
powder that could be mixed with water to make milk. Many were
fearful and refused it. The Lord gave me peace that I was in His
hands, and I drank it thankfully. Then the soldiers began trying
to distribute vitamin pills. There had been no vitamin pills in
Europe before the war, and the Jewish prisoners were too suspicious to take them. I kept thanking God and took anything.

151

It was difficult for the British soldiers and officers to understand the reactions of the prisoners. After all we had been through at the hands of the SS, it was impossible for a Jew not to feel panic at the sight of a man in uniform approaching. It was very difficult to trust the kindness of these soldiers, not to believe that it would ultimately be a ruse. Had not our people gone to the very doors of the gas chambers believing in the assurances of officers?

After a few days the British brought us canned meat. They were desperately anxious to help us. I was too weak to open my can of meat. I just held it and looked at it. Around me starving people were tearing off the tops and devouring the meat. It was God's mercy that I could not open my can, because many died from that feeding. It was too much for their bodies after such a long time of starvation. I had my Bible and my can of meat, and I held them both and looked at them. I could open neither.

I was still in the barracks, and there were far more dead than alive around me. I wondered if I would die still holding my two possessions. But in another day or two I was carried out of the barracks on a stretcher. I remember being stripped of my lice-infested garments. Even my Bible was taken away, but I no longer cared. Then I was sprayed with DDT. I didn't know what it was, but I thought it would be a temporary help and that in a few days all the eggs of the lice would hatch and the insects would be as terrible as before. I wanted to explain to them about the eggs, but I couldn't speak. I was wrapped in a clean blanket. There were ambulances everywhere, and the stretchers soon filled them. The attendants were very kind and I found out they were Quakers, not soldiers, and did only medical work. As we waited, I managed to ask one of them for a piece of paper. I wrote a note to one of my brothers in America. I remembered his name and his house number and another part of the address. I couldn't remember it all. And then I wrote to the Millers' mission in New York, but again I could not remember the address. God performed a miracle with those notes, because both were delivered to the Red Cross headquarters and then from hand to hand, until finally somehow both letters reached their destination.

There were no hospitals for such immense numbers of people, so we were transported to another part of Bergen-Belsen itself, to compounds that had been used by the SS officers.

The Quakers carried us into a huge room with two long rows of mattresses filled with straw. There were neither sheets nor clothing, but we were each covered with a clean blanket.

My typhus worsened and I forgot who I was. I remember once waking up and seeing a German woman with a bitter expression bending over me. I asked her, "Who am I?" and she slapped my face. Later I found out that German women were brought into the camp and compelled to help take care of us, but I never saw this woman again, thanks be to God.

In those days I could think only of God. I couldn't remember who or where I was or what had happened, but I knew that God was with me. I thought of Him all the time, and when I could understand nothing, I could commune with Him. Eventually I was moved to a hospital.

Sometimes I heard a loud thud and later when I asked what the noise was, I was told I had fallen out of bed. Many times I fell. When I came out of my delirium, a British nurse was taking care of me and I asked her for a Bible. Immediately I was given one. It was in English, and I was amazed to have it so easily. But I was still a prisoner in my heart and I hid it under the mattress. Sometimes people asked me my name or the names of my family, but I couldn't remember. God knew my name, and I rested and waited for Him to tell me.

Once an American officer came to see me because he had learned from the nurses that I spoke many languages. He asked me if I would like to be a translator for the military. I was still confused in my mind, and I told him I was going back to my family when I was strong enough. He said nothing, but he did not try to persuade me to work for the military.

Gradually as my mind cleared, I convinced myself that I was the only one in my family who had suffered. I was certain that somehow my doctor brother and his wife and my little brother Joseph and Momma and Felice and her family had gone to America and were alive and waiting for me there. I remembered how our family had talked about emigrating to America, and I thought I could go directly to the United States from the hospital.

Gradually I learned that things were very different now. Those of us from my part of Hungary were informed that our land was now possessed by the Communists. We could not go home, but could be transported to Sweden. I received an identification card to go to Sweden in a "hospital unit."

It seemed to me that in a very short time I would be in the United States and with all my family again!

But at night, in the quietness of the hospital, I heard the Lord say, "Did you ask Me if you should go to Sweden? Did you ask Me if you should go to the United States? It is your wish, but did you ask Me?"

The beloved faces of my brothers, Felice, the tiny figure of Momma in her black dress welled up before me. They were inexpressibly dear. With everything in my heart I wanted to go home. But where was home? And where, really, *were* Momma, and Felice and her sweet-faced little boys and gentle husband? Where were Eugene and . . . something, I remembered something about Joseph . . .

I tossed feverishly on the mattress. I wanted to go home. I *would* go home! But the tender question returned again and again. "Did you ask Me?"

I knew so little then about what had happened. I had seen so much, yet I still understood nothing. I tossed and struggled and saw the eyes of my mother lighten as I came to her and put my arms around her. I pictured Felice overjoyed to see me. We would help one another and grow strong and be all together.

"Did you ask Me?"

Finally I confessed to the Lord that I had not asked Him. I wept. "Lord, I will go where You send me." I was choked with sadness. I did not want to know why the Lord would not let me to go to my family "in America." But there was peace. "I will go where You send me."

The next day I dragged myself out of bed. I had a little strength, and I tried to walk every day. I went to the hospital office and told them I did not want to go to Sweden or America. The Lord also seemed to make it clear that I was not to return to Budapest, to my beloved Hungary. I was to go to Czechoslovakia. My citizenship (but not my heart) had been changed to Czech when I was a little girl. I felt I ought to go to Czechoslovakia.

My mind then turned to the hope that perhaps my family was

there. Perhaps they had somehow weathered out the war in Czechoslovakia.

So the transport to Sweden left without me. As the weeks went by, I did not improve. My impatience grew, but not my strength. I pleaded with the doctor to let me leave on a transport to Czechoslovakia, but he only shook his head and said, "No. You cannot go. You are too sick."

In those days, there were no medicines to be had for the thousands and thousands of Jews suddenly released into freedom. All that could be given to us was rest and shelter and the best food that was available in Germany. But the food was very poor, although to us it seemed like heavenly manna. Once I remember they gave us meat soup. It was either turkey or goose. We didn't need salt, such tears of utter happiness fell into the precious liquid.

On liberation day, my hair had been a prickly stubble. During the typhus it fell out, and I began to wonder if I would ever again have hair. It grew so slowly that even after weeks in the hospital it was only half an inch long, and then stopped growing.

I had been given a ridiculous, brightly striped dress that hung on me as if I were a pole. One day a British officer passed me as I was exercising along the hall, holding onto the wall for support. It was a terrible effort to walk, and I was trembling with weakness and fatigue. As I rested to catch my breath, the officer paused beside me and gave me an encouraging smile. "What a very pretty dress you have!" he exclaimed as he touched the rim of his hat and passed by.

"Action, old goat!" Suddenly years of SS invectives flashed in my mind. I saw myself for an instant staggering through the streets of Essen, my shaved head sticking out of the absurd fur coat. "Scum! Filth! Pig!" I stumbled back to my mattress and turned my face to the wall. In that fleeting gallant moment, the British officer had made me a woman once again.

Transports came and went and still I was in that hospital, unable to gain weight and strength. I was becoming desperate to find my family, to be reunited with them all. Always the French doctor said "No." Finally as I pleaded with him, he asked me to write a note in English to those who would be in charge of the hospital transport. The note was to say that I was very ill and could only travel lying down. I was to keep this note with me at all times and to show it to whoever was in charge.

I was overjoyed! I prepared a little bundle of gifts I had hoarded for my family: a large chocolate bar and a little jam and salt I had managed to save. The hospital moved me to the depot. When I saw the transport, I was very thankful that the French doctor did not know what it was like! There was no way anyone could lie down. The train was ancient, with nothing but wooden benches. The compartments were torn up. I didn't care! I was going home!

Everyone on the train had been a prisoner. Now all were gripped by hope. There was an air of intense patience throughout the long journey. People didn't complain about the many stops, the long delays, the overcrowding. We traveled with our hearts miles ahead of the train and our bodies straining to catch up with them.

We had begun the journey with joking and little songs. People talked happily of the relatives they would soon be seeing and told stories about them and their homes. But as the train passed through cities completely devastated, burned countryside gaping open from bombs, conversation stilled and people's thoughts turned inward with anxiety. Sometimes we stopped at English military bases for the night, where we were given food and water and helped to rest and clean up.

Some of the officers in these British bases were Jewish. I stared at them almost disbelieving. They were Jewish, in the officers' uniforms of their own country! It was wonderful. They were enormously kind to us and entered the train talking, encouraging. All of us carried a document which listed the place where it was permitted for us to leave the train. We could end our journey nowhere else. No one could continue on the train beyond the point written on the document. We all understood this.

The Jewish officers paid no attention to our papers. They were talking to those of us who were the strongest, but all listened with amazement. "Who of us would like to go to Palestine?" they asked. "Jews by the thousands are building a new life for themselves in our original homeland. There you will be among our own. There you can build up Palestine for the Jews and someday . . ."

My heart almost burst with the prophetic words! Had I not

told the women in the bunkers that God had promised that His people would return to the land? And now these British officers were sitting among us, promising to take anyone who wished to Palestine. They would be smuggled in, in spite of the British Mandate that strictly controlled Jewish emigration. Many people wept. I sobbed with a strange joy and wondered if my mind had gone again and I was imagining what I heard. But when the train started up again, there were empty places.

As our journey continued, I became progressively more weak and ill. I had to lie down. To help me, some girls lifted me up to the luggage shelves. I was so thin, there was room enough for me to lie on top of the luggage and still not touch the ceiling of the train. So I traveled in that way.

We passed through the city of Ohlmütz. My destination was Bratislava, where I dreamed I might find my mother and sister. Eugene had once moved to Ohlmütz and had practiced medicine in the hospital there! The train stopped. People were getting off and on. I was seized with the compulsion to get off the train and try to find Eugene. The temptation was immense. I grasped anyone who got into our car. Did they know of a Doctor Warmer? Had they been to the hospital in the city? I described him: he was bald, had large gentle eyes, was 5'10".

I was almost mad with anxiety. Perhaps my brother was in that very city! Someone might know him. I had to get off, to find my few things, to go to Eugene. But no one had heard of him. As I was trying to get off, the train lurched forward with its cargo of hope and it was too late. The Lord had prevented me from making a terrible mistake. Finally we arrived in the city of Prague. I was taken with many others to the Jewish Agency there. Each of us received new clothes and a certain sum of money and a new document for identification. Also at the agency was a list of Jewish survivors. My own name was on the list. It looked strange and somehow frightened me. I wanted to remain as anonymous as possible, to keep out of notice, to stay in the middle of the crowd. Many times I was still thinking like a prisoner!

My eyes raced over the crumpled pages of names. Momma? Eugene? Joseph? I tore through the file. Felice? I had so many relatives: aunts, uncles, cousins. Over and over I turned the

157

pages. Nothing. There must be other lists. There must be mistakes. A worker gently took the pages out of my hands. I was shaking violently. There was not one name of anyone in my family. Only my own name was listed as a survivor.

"The lists are not conclusive," the worker said, "Every day we are adding names." And taking them off, I thought. I remembered the many in our own hospital who had given their names and then died. "You must get back on the train," the worker said. "You must continue to your destination. You understand. It is not possible to have accurate files." The worker forced me into the street. I don't remember getting onto the train.

I had been so sure the Lord was taking me back to my family! The train wheels no longer sung to me as they sped through the ravaged countryside. My heart was lead, and it took all the strength I had to lift it up to the Lord. I arrived in Bratislava in the middle of a Saturday night. The railroad station was in pandemonium. Russian soldiers, male and female, were everywhere. They had liberated Czechoslovakia from the Germans, but it seemed to me *they* were liberated from civilization and decency. They were jumping on and off the freight cars, shooting their guns, shouting, dancing, drinking, stealing. People were rushing everywhere to get out of their way, and the confusion and chaos was a nightmare.

In a short time, everyone who pushed off the train with me was gone. Some had lived in the city and were making their way to what they hoped were still their homes. Others had been actually met by relatives or friends. I was so depressed and weak, I just sat down on the pavement beside the train. I didn't care about all the screaming and running. I took my little bundle and put it under my head, committed myself to the Lord, and fell asleep. I absolutely didn't care what happened to me.

The Lord guarded me in that station. I learned later that the Russians stole anything they could get their hands on. Many in that Bratislava station were abused and mistreated, but I was not harmed in any way or even awakened!

Early the next morning, I pulled myself to my feet and ventured out of the silent station. I had visited Bratislava years before, but I didn't know the city and had no idea where to go or what to do. I could smell the Danube and hear the screaming of gulls as I made my way through the freshness of the Sunday morning. The streets were already filling up with people. Everyone looked thin and sick to me. But when they saw me, they averted their eyes from my painful shuffle and my bald head and gaunt face.

I breathed deeply. I was almost giddy with the sensation of freedom, of being alone—utterly, blessedly alone. I lifted my eyes to the hills around Bratislava. Ancient castles still rose imperially above the desolation of the city. The spires of a magnificent cathedral flashed in the early sun. But everywhere in the streets was rubble, and the taste of dust and brick filled my mouth and nose.

How in such a great city would I find any of my family? A bell began to toll faintly in the distance from a tower I could not see. I stopped the next person who passed me. The woman was startled and drew back from me, but she listened. I was so excited I could barely speak. "Can you tell me where I might find the closest Baptist church?"

"It's just around the corner!" This woman smiled in relief and hurried away. I marveled at how easily she walked.

Just around the corner! I could manage that far! They had already begun the early service when I arrived. I slipped in and took a seat in the last row. I thought no one would notice me! I was thinking, "I am so small and inconspicuous. I could even lie on top of the luggage on the train shelf."

They were singing. In my student days I had heard the finest choirs in Europe. I had been transported by the greatest musical works in the history of Western civilization. Many times I had been moved to tears, the engraving on my elegant programs blurred by the beauty that carried me into emotions and experiences that were deep in my soul.

But in that wooden Baptist hall, those wavery voices moving through a hymn to my blessed Savior overwhelmed me. My hands shook terribly. I tried to reach for a hymnbook. I was unable to pay attention to what I was doing. I wept uncontrollably. After so long! I was afraid someone would think I was a crazy person. I pulled my Bible out of my little bundle and held it in my hands, almost in the same way I as a student had held my admission ticket to the concerts so the attendants would know I had paid.

159

A kind sister slid along to the pew where I was sitting and got a hymnal for me and found the place. Tears kept streaming down my cheeks. She knew I could not read or sing, but I think she wanted to be kind and make me feel welcome and encouraged. I was shaking my head, trying to compose myself. It was so blessed to be there.

After the service the people gathered around me, and the pastor came and spoke with me. I told them my story and asked everyone about my family.

The faces around me were filled with love and tenderness. Tears were pouring down my cheeks again. I was so thankful to be among Christian brothers and sisters after so long. But no one had heard of my family.

As we were talking, the choir began to practice at the front of the hall for another service. People desperately wanted to help, to be able to give me any information, but heads shook helplessly. All the names I could pull out of my memory I dragged forth. Old neighbors, tradespeople, family friends, anyone that might have had some contact with them. Finally I thought of the pastor who had baptized my sister Felice after her conversion. The pastor's face was instantly transfixed with amazement.

"His daughter is here! In my choir!" A commotion ensued! The startled girl was rushed from the choir to my side. I clung to her as my last hope. She assured me her father was at home. She would take me to him. We could ask him if he had any news of Felice and her family.

I was in a frenzy of excitement. Her home was not far from the church, but the distance seemed immense. I could barely concentrate on polite conversation with the girl, I was so intent to get to her father.

When we finally arrived at her home and the father was brought before me, I was suddenly afraid. He was a good, gentle man, and joyful that I had survived the terror of the camps. I must have the best chair. Tea must be brought immediately. I must rest after such a long journey and such an uncomfortable night. I felt my eyes staring at him in a mad way. I tried to speak, to ask him about Felice, but I was suddenly so weak I wondered if I could stand a shock if he had one to give me.

The daughter understood. With a soft look in my direction, she put her hand on her father's arm to halt his welcome.

"Poppa, Sister Rose is looking for her family." The girl spoke in a quiet, calm voice. "You remember baptizing her sister, Felice . . ." The daughter was sitting me down, now lightly resting her hand on my shoulder.

I couldn't bear to look at the man. I was choking with apprehension. I clenched my hands and fixed my eyes on them. My fingers surprised me. They were like twisted sticks. I wanted a window opened.

The man's voice melted in tenderness. "Felice is alive, Rose! Felice is well! And the boys and Alexander, Rose!" The man was at my chair, shaking me gently. "Your sister is well! I can take you to her. It is not far. Just a few villages away!"

It was too much. I wept with relief. My head swam. I grasped my little bundle, shaking with joy. There was no time for the tea. No time for courtesy. We must leave now. How we got out of the house and into the car and to my sister's city I don't remember. I couldn't think, I couldn't talk. I was overwhelmed with happiness. After all that had passed, I would be again with my family.

When we approached the house I was trembling violently. Felice herself answered the door and stared apprehensively at the odd group of people on her threshold. Her eyes locked with mine. In an instant she gave a great cry and caught me in her arms. The pastor helped us both into the house. Felice's children were afraid of me, but accepted the chocolate and called me "Auntie Rose" as before.

Felice was frighteningly thin and unwell herself. She was hardly able to be on her feet, yet she was the older sister still and made me go to bed. It was true that I was exhausted and that the journey and the emotion had made me ill again. But I was delirious with questions. How had they all survived? Where was Momma? Where were Eugene and his family, and Joseph? I wanted to know everything.

Felice soothed me as if I were a baby. I had to rest. I was very ill. I had had a long journey. I had already had too much excitement. She would tell me everything. She would tell me about everybody. But for now, I had to be quiet. I had to get my strength back.

It was not possible to argue with Felice. I had never been able to coax her to do anything she thought unwise in all our growing up years. However I might storm or plead or wheedle, Felice's good sense was her fortress. Now she smoothed my blanket and told the boys to kiss me good night. Auntie Rose was going to sleep and rest and eat and get strong. Everything in good time.

I awoke in a temper. Where was Momma? I was not well, and Felice would not tell me the simplest news. I had a right to know about the family. When could I see Momma? Where was she? Felice was carrying her nursing and mothering too far. The worry would make me sicker.

Felice had been so overjoyed to see me, she had not stopped smiling since I arrived at her house. Now her face grew so changed, I was gripped with fright. She looked hard at me. Tears rimmed her eyes. I wanted to stop her words before they were uttered, to raise my hand and push back what I knew she was going to say. But I couldn't move or speak. I just stared back at her in horror.

"My darling little Rose . . ." I was shaking my head. I did not want to hear. Felice hesitated, then went on. "Rose, please, we will talk about it later. When you are stronger."

So I knew my mother was dead.

We didn't talk about it at first. I didn't ask for a few days about anybody else, and Felice said nothing. I woke up in the nights sobbing and scorched with fever. During daylight hours, we pretended I did not know. I rested, ate, watched the little boys play. Felice and Alexander, now frail and worn, spoke cheerfully of simple things. It was possible now to buy bread. The weather was fine. I would walk outside soon. Did I think it possible that the children had grown so much?

I didn't question God. I had learned to trust Him and to know He is our loving Father. Over and over I reminded myself that He gave His only begotten Son for me, a sinner. He died on Calvary's cross for me. I knew He loved me. He loves all His creation. Day by day as I rested and grew stronger, I tried to rest also in the Lord and prepare myself for hearing all that Felice would have to tell me.

Her story came first. Because they were Christians and had a Bible and went to church, Felice and Alexander had thought in

162

the beginning that they would be spared the camps. For some time they lived in this hope. Mother was seventy-five and not well, so it was not too difficult to hide her, and there was hope that their little family would be overlooked in the terrible deportations.

It was a foolish dream, and one day a neighbor raced to their house to tell them that they were being sent to the camps. "You must flee!" The voice at their window was gone as suddenly as it had come.

In frantic terror Felice and Alexander and the boys and Momma fled to the mountains that circled their town. How does one rush two frightened little boys and an aged, ill woman who can barely walk? But somehow they made it to the mountains and to the camp of some partisans who were waging a guerrilla war against the occupying German forces.

The little boys were recovering from minor surgery, and Momma was barely able to move. It was bitterly cold, but the mountains were full of Jews fleeing the Nazis. There was no room for anyone to shelter at the partisan camp. The partisans had suffered terrible losses and were in the process of retreat. So after their escape from the city, Felice's weakened little family had to remain on the open mountain, hiding among the trees. There was nothing to eat. Eventually, among the Jews hiding in the mountains, Felice found an old cousin of mother's who had a little grain, and who knew where other distant members of our large family were hiding. Felice brought them together into one group. But mother and her aged cousin could not travel. They were too old and ill. There was great distress. Survival depended on mobility. What could be done?

Finally the family found a small cave and tried to make it comfortable for mother and her cousin. They could hide safely there with some food and water. The Nazis would complete their operations in the city, and when the terror was over plans could be made to return.

Even if the Nazi bands who continuously searched the mountains came upon two harmless elderly ladies in the cave, my relatives thought they would surely leave them alone.

Felice had no choice. To stay in one place meant certain death for the group. Mother and her cousin wanted to rest in the cave and wait for the Nazis to go on to some other town. Felice wept at the incredible naivete that could have left two old women to the mercy of the SS. Mother and her cousin were found and routed out, along with Gentile partisan families in hiding, and all were taken to Ravensbruck. To think of my frail mother packed in a camp transport was almost unbearable to me. Felice learned from a woman who was with my mother that when the trains were unloaded at the camp, the SS ordered all Jewish girls and women to step forward. There were no papers in that great mixed crowd of people, and it was possible to hide.

Mother spoke German beautifully and did not look Jewish in the least. But when the call came for Jewish girls and women, Momma stepped forward along with the others. It would not have occurred to her to pretend she was Aryan. Momma was immediately sent to the gas chambers.

For a long time, Felice thought mother was safe and had returned with her cousin to the city.

For almost six months, Felice and her husband and boys hid in the high mountains, running ahead of the Germans, many times being within a hairsbreadth of being shot down. One day Felice found some warm children's clothing in the forest. It happened that the clothing was uniforms of Hitler's Youth Party. Even so, Felice, always practical, thanked God and dressed her twins in the Nazi uniforms.

Some time after finding the clothing, a Nazi squad found Felice and her family camping on the side of the mountain. They were immediately arrested and taken with other fugitives to the prison in the nearest city. Felice protested that she and her family were Christians. They had no papers, so the SS had nothing to prove that this was a Jewish family. But so obsessed were the SS that no one with any Jewish blood could be permitted to live, that they removed the twins from Felice for questioning.

One of the boys was brought before a tribunal of officers for questioning. He was only five or six years old. Felice was in agony, but had to pretend to be waiting confidently for his release. She and her husband well knew that all their lives depended on what that tiny boy would say.

The officers were apparently amused by the courage of my little nephew. He stood without crying before them. They began

164

to mock him and asked him why he stood so straight. The child mocked in return. Why did the officer stand so straight, then? Then the officer laughed and made a face. My nephew made a face in return. I think he was so frightened, he didn't know what to do except copy what the officers did. Finally one of the officers leaned down to him and whispered, "Tell me the truth. Are you a Christian or a Jew?"

The child didn't hesitate. "I am a Christian. We are all Christians!" My nephew made his declaration with such indignation, the officers laughed. The truth was, the child too was in agony. He knew that Jews were shot, but because his fear came out in such force, the SS thought he was a wonderful comedian and let him go.

The officers could have easily seen for themselves if he was circumcised, but the Lord prevented them from thinking of it.

Being free from the prison did not mean that my sister's family had any place to go. They couldn't return to the town, where they would be reported as Jews. There was nothing to do but return to hiding in the mountains. Until liberation, they lived in constant flight and hunger. There wasn't a moment in all those months that they were not starving or in instant danger of being discovered by the German squads patrolling the mountain. Many times people hiding with them were discovered and shot. They learned to run through a rain of bullets, to be ready at a second's notice to plunge through the forest, away from the pounding horses of the SS.

I gazed at Felice's worn face as she told me these things, and noticed for the first time how very frail and quiet the little boys were. Felice's husband, too, was skin and bones. "It is hard for the children to relax." Felice's anxious eyes turned to her sons who were playing silently in a corner of the room. I understood her illness and the circles under her eyes. For months after liberation, she had to stay up every night so that when the little boys awoke, sobbing with old terrors, they saw her and would go back to sleep.

We put our arms around each other. There was so much to say, yet we were both afraid, not sure how much each of us could bear. When she wasn't smiling, Felice looked haunted. I knew she was carrying unspeakable secrets.

"Eugene?" I could hardly bear to ask.

Felice closed her eyes.

"Joe?" I whispered the name.

Felice's eyes remained closed. She was absolutely still. "Rose, you and I are left. You . . . and I."

Later I learned that my beloved Eugene had worked as a doctor in the camps, as starved and ill as the Jewish prisoners he served, doing what he could to ease their agony. One day there was a mass evacuation of his camp to make room for new arrivals. The old prisoners were marched to Auschwitz. During the deportation march, he suffered an attack of angina. His heart pain was so intense he staggered, doubled over in the line, and was unable to keep up the relentless trot at which prisoners were always forced to advance. An SS officer saw him lagging and ordered him to run. When he couldn't, he was simply shot on the road.

Eugene's nurse wife and beautiful children already had perished at Auschwitz.

For days I could think of nothing but the terrible things done to my family. In my spirit I clung to the Lord. I reminded myself of all His mercies, and I knew that we should love Him with all our hearts and walk with Him and do His will. But my mind was in the grip of horror. The sights and sounds and smells of the camps tormented me anew. I thought of our family's children, Eugene's little girls, our old relatives, all the faces and voices that had perished. Altogether, on both sides of our family, 180 relatives had died.

After that time with Felice, it was many years before I could even speak of those things without choking with tears and confusion. I have learned that I must leave them with God. I can tell of the things He did for me and how He helped me carry my burdens in those camps. He is the God of all comfort and He is mother and father, brother and sister to all those who trust in Him. This is what I learned to say to those who were left, who like me had to try to live again after such experiences.

We all knew that to be a Jew and be alive was a miracle. But surviving did not mean the end of suffering. It was a continuation of it. Even Gentiles who had lasted out the war in their own villages and cities were suffering. There was almost no food to be bought at any price. Shops were devastated or deserted. People

166

appeared in the streets in outlandish clothing; anything that could be acquired was gratefully put to use. Fit or style mattered nothing. Women gladly wore men's coats. Children wore anything. Everyone was hungry or ill.

I stayed with Felice a long time. She had put me to bed the moment I arrived in her home, and weeks passed before I could get up. The camps had left me with a damaged heart and high blood pressure. The headaches and back pain from beatings continued, and it was difficult for me to walk.

I spent the days studying the Word of God and praying. Life was so difficult for me. I could barely drag my body around. In the days, pain never left me. In the nights, I would awaken, sobbing terribly from some dream of horror. Yet I had my sister and her family. I had a bed and rest and shared in what food there was. Above all, I had the Lord Jesus and His Word.

But what about those thousands from the camps who had nothing but their bones? How my heart broke for them! They were my people and they needed God more than ever. In the camps, prisoners survived on hope. Hope that they would outlast the war and find again a beloved father or child or husband or mother or wife. But liberation for most meant the end of any reason to go on living. That one loved person for whom anything was endurable had perished!

What did those people do in the black nights when they awoke from their nightmares alone? Who was with them to give them comfort and meaning? How could they bear their sufferings and memories without God? I became more and more restless. I had to leave Felice and her family. I had to go into the city and share the Scriptures with my suffering people.

Felice was aghast. For one thing, the streets were filled with Russian soldiers. They were violent and lawless, and no one was safe. Even old women were raped and sometimes killed. Everybody knew the Russian phrase *"Davay Chasiy,"* which means "Give me your watch!" The Russians took everything, and there was not an undamaged house that did not have to board soldiers. There were no beds to be had anywhere. For a woman alone in the city, it was not possible to be safe.

And my health! What foolishness. Even if I found a bed, how would I manage? It would take all my time just to find food. And how would I have the strength to cook it? Even the money given to me at the Jewish Agency in Prague meant almost nothing. Peasants would not sell food. It could only be exchanged for goods. The Russians would take everything I had, and I would be left ill and with no food or money. Felice wept and pleaded with me. Why did I always have to be crazy? Even the camps had not changed me!

But I felt I had to go. With the money I had I was able to buy some vegetables. We had an old rucksack, and I filled it with vegetables and strapped it on my back. The Lord had not saved me from the camps to lie in my sister's bed!

VIII

Wilderness
Wandering

WHEN I ARRIVED in Bratislava, I saw immediately that Felice's grim description of the situation was not exaggerated. Coarse Russian
soldiers were everywhere, and the townspeople
were fearful and unfriendly. Since there was only one
place in the city I knew, I set off straight for it—the
Baptist church. When the pastor's wife saw me, she was dis-
mayed. "Rose, you should never have come to the city! The
soldiers have taken everything. It is impossible to find a bed.
What will you do?"

It was not an enthusiastic welcome. Still I tried to take heart. I
told her that the Lord had called me to the city. It was not my
idea. I was to witness and distribute Scripture to the Jews who
like me had survived the camps. It was true that I had nowhere to
go, and no Scriptures to give, but that was in God's hands.

A slow smile lit her face. She stared at me for a few moments,
and then led me to the basement of the church. I can still see her
watching and smiling as she told me to open a big box stored
there. It was filled with Hebrew New Testaments—small blue
books, prophecy editions, printed in America by the Million
Testament Campaign. They had been left at the church by Mr.
and Mrs. George Davis, of the Million Testament Campaign. I

had heard of this couple from Karl and the Millers at the Budapest mission. In the mission we had often prayed for them. And here was their great supply of Hebrew New Testaments waiting to be distributed.

I could not read Hebrew in those days, but I knew the Scriptures were a confirmation from the Lord. Joy flooded my body!

For the first days in Bratislava, I stayed here and there in the apartments of people in the church. A seamstress let me sleep in her bed with her for a few nights. Then someone else would offer a couch or some cot in a spare corner "until something came along," and in this way the Lord provided for me. It might have been embarrassing for people to have me coming and going in their crowded homes, if they had not been full of love for the Lord. The fact was, I looked a sight.

The only coat I had was an ancient one Felice had found for me. It had been given to her when she was about to deliver the twins because her own coat wouldn't button up and keep out the cold. The coat was huge, and did well for Felice in her enlarged condition. I could have wrapped it around myself three times!

Unfortunately, I still had no hair and so I kept my head covered. I had found an old felt hat, and I wore it day and night. People couldn't tell if I was a man or a woman, and it was in this condition that I started my work for the Lord.

I soon found out that even though Mr. and Mrs. Miller and Karl had been forced to leave Hungary, they had by no means forgotten Europe, nor had they forgotten me. In those terrible war years, Mr. Miller had raised up many people in America to pray for me. Over and over at his meetings he would tell the story of the Jewess, Rose, who loved Jesus and who he felt sure would have been taken to a camp. The Millers didn't know if I was alive or not, but they prayed for me, and Karl prayed, and many people I did not know at all prayed faithfully for me, month after month.

In later years, many of these same American people came to me and told me that countless times they thought it was useless to pray any longer. Reason told them that I would have surely perished like so many thousands of others, but the Holy Spirit would urge them to continue praying and so they did.

I wrote the Millers in America, and soon I began to get letters and little gifts of money from these praying people who knew of the work I was trying to do and who wanted to help me. I was deeply moved by such wonderful encouragement. I was astonished at the way the Lord had undertaken to help me.

I wrote to tell the Davises that I was using their Scriptures. Almost sooner than it seemed possible, a food parcel arrived from them. My brothers in America, Louis and Herman, sent me food. Karl steadily sent boxes of beautiful used clothing. Not only did I have enough to eat in that starving city, but I had food and clothing to share! In those days that was a tremendous thing!

I was spending a lot of my time translating English tracts. There was nothing available in any of the European languages, and the need for Christian literature was very great. People were eager to read. They wanted to find answers for their ravaged lives, but there was nothing to give them. With the small gifts of money, I was printing tracts and giving them away. I even managed to order some New Testaments in European languages from London, and the Davises sent special orders for me to the Beatenberg Bible School nearby—boxes of New Testaments and tracts and booklets.

I prayed over each tract! And many of the people at the Baptist church supported me with their prayers and their willingness to help. Christians had nothing to give except their prayers and their efforts, but that was everything! Czechoslovakia was cleaned out. Nothing of value was left to anybody. First the Germans had ransacked it. Then the liberating Russian army stripped it bare. People had to stand by helplessly. If Russian soldiers in a home wanted fuel to boil water for tea, it was nothing for them to pull out a drawer and smash it for firewood. Just for a cup of tea!

Misery was on every face.

Yet here I was, in God's grace, a camp survivor with nothing, giving away food and clothing, setting up a little printing business, buying paper and envelopes and stamps and what I needed as the Lord provided. It was miraculous, and people were astonished at what the Lord could do!

I knew I needed a place to live. I was still going around from home to home, and it was a great inconvenience to everyone. I was trusting the Lord and telling Him my needs as the Scriptures command. I couldn't look for a room to rent because even if one were available, it was an impossible luxury for one person to have a whole room.

One day the pastor of the Baptist church hurried to see me. His eyes were twinkling. He had an acquaintance, a Salvation Army woman officer who had worked for a long time in Bratislava. She had a furnished apartment in the city. She was being transferred to Brünn to a higher position in the Army, and she needed someone trustworthy to take care of her apartment in Bratislava. There was a young man, an invalid, who had to stay in the flat. She wanted someone who could come to help him and at the same time stay in the apartment and look after it for her.

Did the pastor know anyone?

The flat had two rooms and a very large kitchen and storeroom. There was a single faucet in the kitchen. I used to turn it on and watch the water run out according to my wishes. Once I had fought with hundreds of people for a drop of water from a faucet, and here I now had a tap all to myself!

A few days after I had moved into the flat, I was at the Jewish Agency in Bratislava waiting in line for something. Behind me was a young woman who peeked around my shoulder to see if I were a man or a woman! We began talking. Her name was Irene, and she was the only survivor in her whole family. They had all been taken to Ravensbruck, the same camp where my mother was killed. Irene had escaped by jumping out of a window of her barracks when all the women in her block were ordered to the gas chambers. I saw she had nothing and no one. I invited her to share the bed I had in the big room of the flat. She lived with me for two years before she professed the Lord. I shed many bitter tears over her, because she would agree and pretend to believe, but still continued on in her own will. But eventually she came to truly accept Jesus as her Savior.

In the weeks and months to come, many Jews and Christians came to sleep in that flat. Often visitors would attend the Baptist church and when they asked the pastor where they could find lodging, where a hotel might be (there were no hotels left in Bratislava), the pastor would grin and send them to "Hotel Warmer."

Often they would have to sleep on the kitchen floor on blankets, but we managed, and I was able to serve the Lord by

172

just bringing people in who had nowhere else to go. Sometimes the guests were Jews who had survived the camps and told me their stories. Everyone had such terrible stories, but each Jew who survived was a miracle, and each was eager to describe his escape or survival.

I learned that some people hid Jews for money. I came to know a lovely Jewess called Stephanie who was eleven years older than I. Although people charged fantastic prices for hiding Jews, it was also true that they risked their own lives to do it. Stephanie was hidden by a woman who demanded all of her money and possessions. Others were with Stephanie in hiding. During the day, the woman hid the Jews in piles of bedding. They had to lie absolutely still all day. But at night she made them work hard, scrubbing the floors and cleaning, in spite of the fact that they were paying a fortune for their stay!

Stephanie's husband had been killed, and she was desolate and longing for a reason to go on living. We were only a month into what came to be a lifelong friendship when Stephanie gave her life to the Lord.

But there were so many survivors of the holocaust. How could I find them? I was only one woman with one voice. It is true that the voice could speak in many languages, and this was of great use. But Europe heaved with mass movements of people. Everywhere people were searching for their lost ones, their homes. Since the Nazis had torn whole populations out of their homelands, refugees of many languages mingled in the streets. I discovered I could talk to almost anyone. I had German from my father, Hungarian from my childhood, the hated Czech of my schooldays, French lessons from Mademoiselle, the English learned during my flight from Louis, the Russian of my missionary work before going to the camps.

But only one voice! There had to be a way of telling all these brave Jews that there was yet meaning in life. They had to know that the ancient prophecies had come to pass and Jesus was Messiah! I agonized in prayer. One day I happened to hear that the names of all the Jews who had returned to Slovakia were contained in three big books, each the size of a telephone directory.

I was electrified! It was possible to write down the names. To obtain addresses. Tracts could be mailed all over the country to these dear people who had suffered so much. Did I not know how they had suffered? Did I not share their memories, their night-mares, the sounds and sights that filled their conscious hours? I could give them the Word of God! I could speak, through tracts, to each of them! I could send them the New Testament.

It was not easy to share my vision with those around me. Everyone was poor. All the work that was done was done on thin air. People didn't even have shoestrings! But the Christians at the Baptist church were willing to pray. The people in the United States who knew me prayed. Karl and the Millers prayed. Even people in Canada who knew about me through the Millers were praying for my witness to the survivors in Slovakia.

But money was needed for stamps. New Testaments and liter-ature in the many languages of Europe needed to be bought. Envelopes to carry this precious message were needed. The task seemed immense.

In the meantime, a wonderful thing happened. My beloved American Mary returned! As soon as the borders were opened, she was one of the first missionaries to return, as fresh and radiant as ever and overjoyed to see me alive. She came to Bratislava because her orphanage was in Russia, and doors to that land were now firmly closed.

Mary was undaunted. She would open an orphanage in Brati-slava then. With what? Mary only smiled. Wherever she went, whatever she planned to do, things moved fast. She knew how to touch the heart of people for children, but most of all she knew by prayer and intercession how to touch the heart of God.

The progress of Mary's orphanage was another miracle, be-cause people had almost no possessions left even for themselves. But before long, Mary had enough blankets and clothes and dishes gathered together to begin a little orphanage for the war orphans nobody wanted. Often when she was in the city, she came to visit our flat with a little group of her children.

The flat became more and more like a hotel, with people coming and going. The young invalid had recovered and left, but one day the Lord sent a Child Evangelism missionary from Canada to visit and she stayed on. Irene was still with me, and Margaret, the Canadian missionary, made our apartment the base for her work. She brought with her visual aid materials for the children, but they were so new that young people and grown-ups were fascinated and her meetings were well-attended. I learned to use visual aids from Margaret.

Somehow there was always room for whomever the Lord sent, and always just enough food for one more. Often people only stayed one night and went on. Sometimes they came and stayed, as did Margaret.

Another Canadian, a Mrs. Gordon, was one of these. She was a very independent woman who had been a secretary for a member of Parliament. In her spare time she distributed Scripture to Jewish homes in Toronto. The Lord laid Czechoslovakia on her heart; so she packed up and came. But it was not possible for her to find any place to live in Bratislava, and so the Baptist pastor said, "Mrs. Gordon, go to Rose Warmer. She needs you."

Mrs. Gordon didn't want to work with me; she wanted to be independent, but in the end she came. She stayed for almost two years and was an immense help. That was the spring of 1947.

By this time the Lord had answered many prayers and used Mr. and Mrs. George Davis and the Million Testament Campaign to provide Scriptures for us in Hungarian, Czech, and German. I spent hours going back and forth to the post office, picking up boxes of literature, Scriptures, and tracts in an old baby carriage that someone gave me, and pushing it back to the apartment.

No one laughed. In those days you could see anything on the street and not be surprised! There was always a logic to it. After the literature arrived at the apartment, we would pray over it. We prayed for every person who would receive even the smallest portion of God's Word. We were so grateful for the praying and giving friends in the United States and Canada. Over and over we thanked God for the Million Testament Campaign. Without the help of this organization, there wouldn't have been Scriptures to distribute at all.

One morning Mrs. Gordon, Irene, Margaret, and I were getting ready for the day in our little apartment. There was a lot of noise in the streets, and we hung out of the windows into our courtyard to find out what was going on.

"The Communists have taken over!" Everyone was shouting and running around, and the streets were overflowing with soldiers. It seemed that there couldn't be more to suffer, but that is always a mistaken idea. More can come, and for us it did! Store owners who were just beginning to manage, and factory owners and business people who had worked so desperately hard to begin again immediately lost everything. Everything was taken from them by the government, and they were left on the streets, penniless and homeless. Disaster fell upon everyone. We had had to line up for food in the shops before the Communist takeover, but now food became much harder to get, and it was of such poor quality that it was hard to digest.

There was general panic, just as there had been when the Nazis took over.

A few mornings after the Communist takeover, there was pandemonium in our courtyard. The yard was overrun with excited soldiers ordering all of us in the flats to throw our possessions, furniture, everything into the courtyard. All of us had to move! There would be three families to every apartment!

Three families! Poor Mrs. Gordon was appalled. She was a gracious lady, and since one of the soldiers knew English, she sweetly tried to dissuade him. I explained hotly that this was not our flat; I was keeping it for another woman and couldn't move out! All the other families were furious at the soldiers and refused to move.

The soldiers had a huge truck ready to move us and two other families. We were all to be moved to one apartment where we would live together. I ran to the authorities, whose office was down the street, but they simply said, "You must obey!" Because the soldiers found the least resistance with us women, since we were two Jews and two foreigners, they forced us into the truck and drove us off. The other families still refused to unlock their doors and obey.

We were taken to our destination, and our kitchen table and mattresses and all our belongings were thrown inside. Then the soldiers left. The apartment from which we had been evicted had two rooms and a primitive kitchen. We had shared bathroom facilities with several other families in an outdoor courtyard toilet. We had one faucet.

The new apartment had a private bathroom with a tub! The kitchen had a large wood-burning stove and a full sink. There were built-in cabinets and three rooms. The windows of the flat opened out to a secluded courtyard.

Life is full of many holy jokes. How we laughed. Because the other families refused to move, the Lord worked through the situation to give us this finer apartment all to ourselves.

We carried on our ministry in our more comfortable circumstances, working long hours every day and sending out literature. Every six or eight weeks, as the Lord sent us funds for stamps and envelopes and for the printing of new tracts, I would load up the baby carriage and begin the long journey to the post office. There were no tramcars and we did not possess a bicycle, so the baby carriage was for us a vital piece of missionary equipment. It wasn't the most cooperative equipment, either. Sometimes the wheels would fall off and run into the road just where the traffic was heaviest. I'd have to dodge the cars, looking for the wheels while the carriage loaded with its precious cargo leaned crazily on the sidewalk.

So many Jewish people read only Hungarian that it was essential that I have God's Word in that language. Every tract we mailed out had the testimony in it of a Jewish man or woman or sometimes a rabbi who had accepted Jesus as Messiah. Always included was the offer of a New Testament. People only had to write me for it. Our joy grew as the mail increased with Jewish people asking for New Testaments.

There was so much to do, and all of us worked with all the strength we had to share the gospel of Jesus Christ. It was often difficult because our food supply was poor and grew worse as the Communist takeover of Czechoslovakia continued. My own health was faltering. Mrs. Gordon had to write to Canada, asking for flour to make some biscuits she could eat. She was losing weight and energy and couldn't manage the terrible bread we had to wait in line for. Sometimes we simply gave up trying to get bread. It took so many hours to obtain one's ration, we wondered if it was worth it. Soap was also sent to us from abroad and in this way, through small parcels to Margaret or Mrs. Gordon or to me, we shared and lived from day to day.

There were other missionaries now in Czechoslovakia. Even though we had been evicted from the flat of the Salvation Army woman, it didn't mean that "Hotel Warmer" had ceased to operate. The pastor simply sent people to our new address. There was a missionary couple from North America who came and begged me to travel with them as interpreter. They knew Russian but no other language. In this way, I was able to journey around the country to some of the Jews who had written to us and visit them personally.

Margaret too was traveling from time to time, taking the gospel to outlying areas and using her visual materials to capture the interest of boys and girls, and many adults too. She encouraged me to use visual aids and I found them wonderfully helpful, especially in my weakened condition. People were still unspoiled by radio and television and enjoyed flannelgraph presentations.

We now traveled in a wooden cart with clumsy wooden wheels. The poor horse dragged us along bumpy roads, and we shook on those boards like dried peas in a pot! Sometimes I had to silently cry out to the Lord for mercy, as headaches split my head as we lurched from side to side in the cart. But we laughed at the hardships, and I trusted the Great Physician for help. There were no medicines or vitamins to be had in the country.

When we had meetings in those towns and villages, people listened to us in rapt silence. We were deeply rewarded for all the discomfort of the journeying. People's hearts were wide open to the gospel, and their gratitude was touching. Often we would go into their homes for a meal.

They gave us the best they had, which was so scant and poor one's heart cried out for what they were enduring day by day. Usually there was only a single pot or dish to a house, and we all ate out of it as we sat around the table. I had been through enough that my fastidiousness was well under control.

It wasn't long after the Communist occupation that the Secret Police began to visit me. All the mail I was receiving—what was the meaning of it? So many letters from America! So many parcels to this address!

One day when I was at home, a member of the Secret Police banged on our door. When he came in, he demanded to know if I had any literature in the Hungarian language; did I have Hungarian Bibles? According to Communist law, Bible literature is "anti-Soviet" and can be construed as a crime, especially if it is received from foreign countries. I couldn't deny that I had it, yet I couldn't tell him. I would have then involved the entire chain of Christians who were helping me.

I lifted my heart in prayer. We faced each other silently. Then I simply went to the cupboard where all the Bibles were stored and flung open the door. "Here is the cupboard!" I declared. He stared at the shelves. There was also a storage cabinet in a sheltered part of the courtyard where more literature was kept.

"Come with me, please!" I ordered and stepped rapidly out of the apartment and into the garden toward the cabinet. When we reached it, I opened wide its doors. All the time I was praying to the Lord for His help. Both cabinets were packed full of New Testaments.

The policeman looked at the shelves with an expressionless face. Suddenly he turned and without a single word went through the gate and out into the street. My knees were shaking as I made my way back into the apartment and shut the door. I was so conscious of the presence of the Lord, I just sat before Him and worshiped and praised Him. He must have blinded the eyes of that policeman. Never again was I questioned about my literature.

But I began to be harassed in many other ways. When I traveled, I was aware that my journeys were watched by the police. Once I was on a witnessing journey near the Polish border of Slovakia. In the middle of the night when I was sleeping at a little inn, I was aroused and all my belongings searched. They accused me of smuggling goods across the border.

The police were also suspicious because so many people were coming and going all the time to and from our apartment. It was like a beehive. Mrs. Gordon became very quick in making biscuits or a little meal for people who came to us all hours of the day and night.

Even though we seldom had time to wait in the lines for food, the Lord took care of us. Some people would spend all night sitting on the curb, waiting for shops to open. The lines were so terribly long. It was hopeless for us. We would have had no time to do the Lord's work. So we gave up trying for the little food that our weekly ration stamps would have provided. Mercifully, parcels came for us from North America, and we were also sent

Army Surplus parcels. My brother-in-law, Alexander, now worked at a flour mill and was sometimes able to give us flour. We gave him canned food for my little nephews in return. Sometimes we were able to get lard, and that was an occasion for celebration!

The United Nations provided a kind of canned cheese. The Slovak people were not accustomed to canned food, and they didn't like to buy it. Often all of us would combine our ration coupons to buy cheese, which was a tremendous supplement. So we managed in those difficult times and were able to share with anyone who came, so faithfully did the Lord take care of us!

On May 1, 1947, there was a great parade in Bratislava to "celebrate" the Communist takeover of the country. We Christians were not celebrating, but many others who thought they would gain by becoming enthusiasts joined in. The goose-stepping of the troops, the rolling of artillery was ominously familiar. Was I living everything all over again? On that day I was taken very ill and had to go to the hospital.

It was a Jewish hospital. The majority of the patients there were suffering, like me, from their treatment in the camps. For six days I was in the hospital, completely surrounded by my own people and able to witness to them about the Messiah. I didn't need stamps and envelopes and long lists of addresses. There wasn't a face there whose eyes had not looked out on terror, and not a drop of blood that was not Jewish!

Without moving an inch, I could talk to the nurses and the doctors. Every day they ministered to the aftereffects of the Nazi slaughter. Their patients were not ill from the diseases they had studied in their medical training. Their patients were the dregs of the crematoria—those few thousand who had not been devoured by the ovens. They had not escaped. Like me, they had only survived.

In that hospital, I told anyone I could about the love of God and how faithful He had been to me. I read the Psalms and the Prophets and told how Jesus is the fulfillment of all the ancient and unfailing promises of Jehovah. The hunger for meaning I had seen in the village meetings, in the mail response to the tracts was all about me. It was a blessed time, in spite of my pain and the immense effort to talk. And in all the wards, in the halls, I was hearing a new kind of talk. It was on the lips of the young girls who delivered food trays to us patients. The women cleaning the rooms discussed it together. Recuperating patients gathered in small clusters and spoke in excited voices. It was talk of Palestine! Our homeland!

I felt a surging in my blood. If it were so wonderful to be in this hospital, surrounded by my people, able to minister without the long and exhausting search for survivors, how would it be to live in Palestine where I would be in the midst of thousands of Jews all the time!

But another word was whispered in anxious tones: the British! The British refused. The British prevented. There was the White Paper.

I had known about the White Paper. Every Jew in Europe knew about it. In 1920 the British, who had been victorious in the Mideast in World War I, had acquired Palestine as a Mandate from the League of Nations. The plan then had been to establish Palestine as a Jewish national home.

Perhaps it had seemed simple at the beginning—perhaps it had never been simple—but the passing of years brought intense conflict to the Mideast. By the thirties, there was a three-way struggle among the Arabs, the Jews, and the British on how this Jewish national home was to be achieved. The powerful Arab nations insisted on halting Jewish emigration; the British decided to limit it severely.

It is difficult to understand, but in 1939, the very year Hitler declared war on the Allies, the British, who were so courageous in combating Hitler, in their own way also declared a terrible war on the Jews. They issued a White Paper announcing Britain's intention to create a single independent state in the Mideast (not a state partitioned into Arab-Jewish zones), and this state would be predominantly Arab. Jewish emigration to Palestine was limited to 1,500 persons a month, and this tiny trickle would end as soon as the Jewish population reached 500,000. Halted forever. The quota had been reached in 1944.

Now angry words were raised in the hospital. What about the British blockade of the ships crowded with Jews now steaming on their way to Palestine? Everyone had been sure that Jews who had stayed alive in Europe would be let into Palestine if they wanted to come. Surely the White Paper would no longer be in effect. Not after what had happened.

But the White Paper was ferociously in effect, and what was happening to those tragic shiploads of Jews was a horror as great as the camps. Zionists in Palestine were opposing the British, making heroic efforts to force the British to permit the landing of the ships. Rumors that guns were hidden in the ships, that the Jews in Palestine were training and arming themselves to help the Jews of Europe come, sent a thrill of pride through my aching head. A state of martial law was said to exist in Palestine.

Although the British army was patrolling the ports and shores of Palestine, Jewish ships were getting through. A doctor told of the teenagers of Palestine, young boys and girls, born free in that land, who were risking their lives on the beaches to ford the waves and wade out to the tiny boats full of survivors from ships unable to dock in any port. Palestinian girls and boys carried in their arms or on their backs frail old people, babies, children, even men to the soil of their homeland, under the very guns of the British.

There would be war, the doctors said. We Jews would win. Palestine would soon be open to any Jew in the world who wanted to come.

I asked the nurse for a cold cloth for my head and a drink of water. I was trembling with emotion. Bible prophecies flooded my memory.

> For there shall be a day when watchmen on the hills of Ephraim shall call out, "Arise, and let us go up to Zion, to the Lord our God." For thus says the Lord, "Sing aloud with gladness for Jacob, and shout among the chiefs of the nations; Proclaim, give praise, and say, 'O Lord, save Thy people, the remnant of Israel.' Behold, I am bringing them from the north country. And I will gather them from the remote parts of the earth, among them the blind and the lame, the woman with child and she who is in labor with child, together; A great company, they shall return here. With weeping they shall come, and by supplication I will lead them; I will make them walk by streams of waters, on a straight path in which they will not stumble."

With all my heart I wanted to help. The thirty-first chapter of Jeremiah and many other passages thrilled me. I felt my spirit was dancing on the dry sands of Palestine!

After six days I went home, little better but with a lot to think about and a lot of work to do. I felt an even greater urgency that our Jewish people should have the Scriptures. If they returned to their prewar homes and villages, if they made new lives for themselves, if above all they went to Palestine in spite of the terrible uncertainties, they needed God's Word.

But my health continued to be poor. As much as I could, I simply ignored my body and carried on with the work.

But only a year later I was back in that same hospital, admitted on May 3, 1948. This time I was a patient for forty days. My blood sugar was high, and I alternated between high fevers and heaving chills. The staff tried all sorts of treatments that were exhausting and ineffective. I knew I was very ill.

So it was that on May 14, 1948, the very day that in faraway Palestine the proclamation of the founding of the State of Israel was declared, I was shaking violently on a thin hospital mattress in the heart of Communist-occupied Czechoslovakia. When the news arrived on shortwave radio at the hospital, there was such cheering that even though I wept with joy, I pressed my hands to the sides of my head. Now it was covered by thin brown hair. No longer the stubble. My ears, so often filled with Nazi curses, were actually hearing Jews proclaiming the founding of the State of Israel, the establishment of a whole nation of the people whose burning bones had blackened the skies of Europe.

I was too weak to move, yet I tried to cheer. I shook with illness and emotion. I held my precious Bible in my hands and wished I had the strength to leap on my bed and shout, "The glory of the Lord shall be revealed! And all flesh shall see it together!" But all I could do was cry and laugh like the others.

At the hospital, talk was of nothing but the war in Palestine. Everyone wanted to go. We knew that Jewish ships were being shelled by the British and taken captive. We knew about the British detention camps for Jews in Cyprus and other places. We knew that Palestinian Jews were now at war with the Arab nations and that the British would be pulling out. Nothing mattered.

It was an unspeakable triumph for each one of us. It was as if at last each of us was personally defying Hitler and our Nazi captors. The Jews would live! The Jews would triumph. Oh, it was glory!

But we were now in a Communist country. News was hard to get. Everything was somewhat censored, and the government severely restricted news about Palestine. Our best source of information was from Palestinian agents who got into Czechoslovakia to spur the young people to join the Palestinian Jews and fight for the liberation of our country.

It was true that these Israeli agents didn't tell *all* the news, either. Only the good news. We didn't hear about the terrible deprivation and problems of the emigrants in those early days. To us, Palestine was the promised land! Many thousands of European Jews were going, we knew. Yet our own borders were closed. The Communists were not permitting emigration to anyone's so-called "homeland."

After I was allowed to leave the hospital, I returned to our apartment with Mrs. Gordon and Margaret and Irene. Often I was so weak and ill I had trouble getting out of bed, but the Lord always raised me up in answer to prayer, and by His grace I was able to continue.

The police harassment made life very hard for us. We were continuing to get food parcels and parcels of clothing. The officials at the post office tried to prevent my collection of the parcels. One day it came to me that they were men with needs of their own and with families. I could see how ragged their shirts and sweaters were, and I gladly gave them some of the clothing in the parcels.

They were not believers, not even Jewish, just people in need, but they became more friendly and lenient. Parcels came to us from the Toronto Jewish Mission and the Cleveland Hebrew Mission. They sent us beautiful clothing, and our souls were filled with gratitude.

About this time, the police began to force me to make detailed lists of all the parcels I received and every piece of clothing in them. Then I had to list again to whom the clothes were given. This was difficult and time-consuming and made the work more tedious.

Irene left about this time, and Mrs. Gordon felt the impossible conditions were the leading of the Lord for her to return to Canada. Our parting was difficult. She had been a wonderful help and friend for almost two years, and we had been through much together. After her departure, Margaret, who was still traveling all over Czechoslovakia, became engaged to a dear Hungarian brother, and they were married. So I was left alone.

The Lord continued to give me many volunteer helpers from the Baptist church and the Brethren Assembly in Bratislava and our work continued, even as conditions worsened. Every Czech Jew was dreaming about emigrating to Palestine, and rumors flew that the Communist Czech government would finally permit legal emigration with rabbis in charge. A Palestine office was established in our town, and even Jews from Hungary (where emigration was not permitted) flocked to this office to apply for return to the land of Israel.

A Palestinian Consulate was set up in Prague, and hundreds of families made the journey from Bratislava to Prague, a trip of a whole night and half a day, to get the papers to emigrate.

Many of the people I had witnessed to in the villages were packing up and getting ready to leave. As I watched them pulling out, my heart followed them, just as it had followed the dear Jewish families I had seen taken from Beregovo to the brick factory. How different it was! Then they were going to destruction. These families were going to a new life. My spirit longed to go with them. These people were my mission field—and if my mission field was moving, then I had to move too! I was praying about it much.

I had learned my lesson in the hospital at Bergen-Belsen when I had planned to "rejoin my family in America." How thankful I was that the Lord had not let me make that terrible mistake. He knew Momma and my brothers had perished. This time I did not want to run ahead of the Lord along a wrong path. But my whole being cried out for Palestine, and I yearned to see its shores. I began to pray for God's guidance.

Felice and her family had been planning to emigrate to America. After the war, my brothers in America went every day to the Red Cross headquarters there for news of me. Both Herman and Louis were doing every conceivable thing to make it possible for us to get out to America. They had provided affidavits for us and had found a job for Felice's husband. An apartment was secured in the United States, and they had tickets for everyone. In the midst of all this, the strain was too great for Louis, and he died suddenly of a cerebral hemorrhage. He was only forty-five years old and left a young wife and a twelve-year-old daughter.

Felice and her husband felt suddenly unsure. Louis's death seemed to shatter their hopes in some way, even though Herman assured them everything would be all right. They were concerned about being a burden on Herman, who had his own family and now Louis's to care for. In the midst of all this uncertainty, my young nephews, now fourteen, declared they were going to emigrate to Palestine. They didn't want to go to the United States—many, many of their friends were going to Palestine.

I was deeply moved by the bravery of my young nephews. There was a rule that all young people going to Palestine went under the protection of an emigration group called "Youth Aliyah." These young people had to go without their parents.

Felice and her husband were shocked. The idea of parting with their children was a terrible thought. Yet the boys were determined to go. Felice and Alexander decided to follow them to Palestine as soon as possible.

It was a sad scene at the Bratislava railway station. Even Mary came from her orphanage to say good-bye to the boys and wish them God's best. We all stood waving and crying as the train pulled away, full of Jewish youngsters. They were in the truest sense our lifeblood, and they were going to a war-torn country where life would be uncertain and difficult. They were so precious a treasure.

Now Felice and her husband, as well as I, longed to get to Palestine. My sister applied for emigration immediately. We were horrified at the Rabbi's response. "You are a Christian and belong to the Baptist church! You cannot emigrate to Palestine!"

My dear sensible Felice looked suddenly wild. Her face drained of any color. I was too stunned to speak. The Lord gave Felice wisdom and courage. When she spoke, her voice had only the trace of a tremble. "What about Ruth, Rabbi? If you say I am not a Jew, then surely Ruth was not a Jew. She was a Moabitess. Yet she said, 'Your people are my people and your God my God,' and she dwelt with the people of Israel!"

The Rabbi looked over his tiny glasses, pondering Felice's forthright question. Her gaze was steady and respectful as she met his. Finally the Rabbi shrugged and wrote her name on his list, and the name of her husband. On the street, we went wild with joy!

Felice and her husband had to sign over their home to the authorities in Czechoslovakia, and had to pledge never to claim it back. Years later they laughed at what they took with them. No one knew what to expect, and Felice's husband took tools and even some wood for building a house, and heavy iron bindings. They were going to Palestine by ship with a large emigration group, and I left them in their village at the end of their preparations and began my own application in Bratislava to emigrate.

But I was refused. I was not a Jew. I was a Christian. I was not only a Christian, I was a missionary. There was no place for me in Palestine. I was appalled. Not go to Palestine? But all the Jews were going there. All my people. Even my family! I couldn't remain in Europe! I was a Jew! Had I not been in Auschwitz? And in the slave labor camps? And in Bergen-Belsen?

Nothing I could say or do changed the minds of the officials. I crisscrossed from one Palestine authority to another. I traveled as far as Prague, but even there I was refused. I didn't know what to do. Day after day I pleaded with the Lord to help me.

The Brethren and Baptist Christians saw my despair. I was rejected by my own people. Believers began to encourage me to go to the United States. My brother Herman was there. There was work to be done among Jews in the United States!

Like Felice, I did not want to be a burden on my brother. He was not a Christian, and I felt he already had a great deal to do to care for his own family. Yet many people in America had prayed for me for years, and many after the war sent money and parcels for my work. Perhaps America was best. But when the time came for someone to sign a guarantee for me, there was no one.

Who wanted a Czech-Hungarian displaced person who was a Jew and a Christian and had survived the horrors of the holocaust, whose health was bad and who was crazy enough to push a baby carriage filled with Bibles along the Communist streets of Bratislava? No one.

How could American Gentiles know the wrenching of my

heart to witness to my Jewish people? How could they understand the stranglehold of the Communist police? How could they imagine the desolation of being the only one left alive in Europe out of a huge extended family? There is a phrase from the book of Job, "I am the only one left." That is how I felt.

In Czechoslovakia, the Communists had already begun arresting and imprisoning ministers and missionaries. There was increasing hostility toward the West, and the United States in particular. I knew that my own arrest was on the way. Every step I took was watched. I became accustomed to being followed. I wondered if I could stand becoming a prisoner once again. There was a grim irony in it all: first to be arrested as a Jew, then as a Christian.

Mary came from the orphanage and tried to help me every way she could. As an American, she thought she might be able to insist that I be given consideration for emigration to the United States. She too was sure my arrest was imminent.

One day a wonderful letter came from a place called Altoona, Pennsylvania, United States. It was from a couple who had been praying for me and corresponding. The man was the owner of a small radio station, and he and I had exchanged tracts by mail.

They encouraged me to apply for a tourist visa to America. Mary was thrilled and said I ought to go ahead. "If you ever get out of this country, Rose," she said with a tender look, "kiss any ground you come to!"

It was her way of saying she understood the terrific pressures that were on me. And I think she felt that I would never survive another imprisonment.

When I took the letter to the authorities, I was lightfooted with hope. Surely now I would be permitted to leave Czechoslovakia! But the authorities were ready for me. I was applying as a Czechoslovakian citizen to emigrate to the United States? Impossible! I was not Czechoslovakian. My citizenship, which had been artificially given to me after I left the camps, had been invalidated by the Communists. I was a stateless person!

All the borders were now closed. I was refused exit to return to my own Hungary and apply for my citizenship of birth. As a stateless person there was nothing I could do. Again and again I went to the Jewish authorities for help. But I was a "bad penny."

188

They turned against me because I had "turned on my own people" by becoming a Christian. I was no longer a Jew.

I was deeply appalled. I had given my whole life to my people! They were everything to me. There was nothing I wanted more in this world than to be with them, to help them, and to share the gospel with them. But the Jewish authorities would not help me. It was terrible. One drop of Jewish blood was enough for Hitler! But a full-blooded Jewess who believed in Jesus was no Jew at all to the rabbis. I was a Christian.

I had nowhere to turn. The Communist police were awaiting their chance to arrest me because I was a Christian. The Jews refused to get me out because I was a Christian. A net was closing around me. I spent my time fasting and in prayer.

The Christians supported me in prayer and did anything they could to show me their love and concern. One day a brother at the church took off his gold rings and said, "Sister, take these. If they will help to get you across the border, sell them and do it." But it would have been useless. Even if I had managed to escape into Hungary, what would I do there? I would still have no passport and no money. And I would know no one. So I kept on praying and pleading with the Lord.

Finally the day came when I submitted to the Lord. "Lord, I don't care. Whatever Your will is . . . Your will be done with me . . . If You want to open the door for me, I will take it gratefully and praise You. Lord, I know if I go through the fire . . . or through the water . . . if I have to die . . . I know I am going to be with You, Lord." I was praising and worshiping God, and He gave me wonderful peace. I knew His will would be sweet to me.

There was a woman, a pastor's wife, whom I used to visit high up in the mountains. This woman knew of my situation and was praying for me. She also knew an influential Secret Police agent. One day shortly after I was at peace, she suddenly went to the police agent on my behalf.

I knew nothing about it. I received an official letter requesting that I appear in the office of the Secret Police. My friends were terribly alarmed. Even Mary was anxious as we prayed together about it.

When I arrived at the office, I was interviewed and told

abruptly that in a few days I was to return to receive a paper. It was mystifying, but I was trusting the Lord. Obediently I returned to the same office at the time I was told. I had spent the days between the two visits waiting before the Lord, thanking Him, knowing that all our Heavenly Father does is good and that His will is the best.

When I arrived, the officer grimly handed me a document. It was a passport! Not a regular one, a stateless passport. But a passport all the same!

I was thanking God all the way to the American Consulate. The official there was a very kind lady, and I thought she would be delighted. When she saw my passport, her face became grave.

"This passport is no good!" She pulled out a visa she had with my name on it. "You have a visitor's visa for America that is good for six months. But I can't stamp it into a stateless passport, because you must have a country to return to!"

Well, I had none. Only my eternal country in heaven.

In the meantime, Mrs. Gordon in Canada had been busy. Because she had worked for a member of Parliament, she went to him and asked him to help get me out. He knew how difficult it was for anyone to emigrate from a Communist country, so he signed some papers and Mrs. Gordon sent me a visitor's visa for Canada, good for six weeks!

Mary went with me, and we took the Canadian visa all the way to the Canadian Embassy in Prague. They said the same thing. "You must have a country to which to return." They were very sympathetic, but there was nothing that could be done.

Prague is one of the most beautiful cities of Europe, but I was exhausted and disspirited. We trudged up and down the hilly streets. I hardly cared where we were going. For once I did not exult in the loveliness of the old section of Prague, or fix my eyes on Hradcany Castle high on a hill overlooking the whole immense city. Mary, as an American, loved it all—the Gothic spire of St. Vitus next to the castle, and on the slope of the castle hill the quaint Mala Strana (lesser town) quarter of Prague.

There were thirteen bridges in Prague, and I began to feel Mary was dragging me across each one of them. She was determined to find the Palestinian Consulate in the city.

I remember standing before a woman official. My head was

aching, my bones groaning from the long walk while Mary pleaded with the Consul. "Look, this woman is a Jewess. She has suffered in a concentration camp. Almost all her family were annihilated because they were Jews. They suffered and died because of their Jewish blood, and simply because this Jewess is a Baptist she is refused a visa to Palestine! Look at her! Help her!"

Mary had such a way with people that this Palestinian Consul meekly promised Mary that I would get a visa to Palestine. We were stunned by Mary's apparent success. There was nothing we could do but hope she meant it, and return somewhat dazed to Bratislava.

But our rabbis in Bratislava took a dim view of the promise made to me in Prague. They were in no hurry to cooperate. Again the weary traveling began, back and forth between the American Consulate in Bratislava to the Canadian and Palestinian consulates in Prague.

Ordinary life was suspended, and I was caught in a web of lines and desperate people at all the consulates where I spent my days. I explained I had the promise from Prague of a visa to Palestine. The American official smiled skeptically. You can't put a stamp on a promise! It was the same in Prague at the Canadian Consulate. Canada was glad to permit my entrance as a visitor, but a stateless passport meant nothing.

Mary insisted I keep returning to Prague. She refused defeat. When we hurried through the drab streets of Bratislava, she would watch the uniformed police with a measured eye. I must continue with my efforts until the Lord gave success in His way.

Those hours in the consulates were not wasted. There were many other Jewish people who were making the exhausting rounds of the consulates too. I was able to witness to them and to give them Scripture and continue my work even there.

At the Canadian Consulate, the workers were very compassionate and tried in many ways to help me get out. They too kept running into difficulties. But Mary insisted that the Palestinian Consul had promised to give me a visa to Palestine, in spite of what the Bratislava rabbis said. Finally the Canadian Consul decided to telephone the Palestinian office and speak herself to the officials.

I was glad to be sitting down. My health continued to be poor, and dragging myself from one place to another in those crowds was very hard. My head was aching. My eyes were swollen with fatigue as I watched the Canadian woman's face as she talked.

Eventually the woman's face, creased in a frown, brightened. She signaled to me with widened eyes. Still speaking, she nodded her head to show there was agreement. I stared at her, hardly daring to believe the message she was communicating. When she hung up, she came around to the front of the desk and shook my hand.

"The Palestinian Consul has promised to send your visa for Palestine to Canada after you arrive. I can give you the visa for Canada!"

It was a miracle! I could go!

Suddenly there was so much to do! I wanted to visit all the old places, all my friends. My feelings would race forward to all the faces I wanted to see one last time. I knew I could never return. Over and over I was seized with an irrational urgency to see Momma, or Joe, or Eugene, or my lost aunts and uncles in Budapest or Vienna.

One last time I went to Mary's orphanage to say good-bye. Mary had done a remarkable work. She had built it up with her own money and the money from people in America, and it was truly beautiful. It was a wonderfully peaceful place in those days of tension and distress, brimming over with love for the Lord Jesus and love for Mary.

I was later appalled to learn that only two days after I left the city, Mary was suddenly accused of being an American spy and was expelled from Czechoslovakia. Her orphanage was wanted. What it cost her to be torn away from her children and to see the Communists moving among them with their workers and their huge pictures of Lenin and Stalin, I can't imagine.

It was like Mary not to return to the United States. She went quietly to Germany and spent two years there, living in camps with displaced persons, helping the refugees from Russia. She gave away everything she had, even her health, until she became as destitute as the refugees themselves.

It was the Lord's mercy that I suspected nothing that was to befall Mary when the day came for me finally to board the train to the West. I was heartbroken to leave Mary and for hours I wept.

But when I came into Switzerland, it was a marvelous thing to breathe the free air of that country! I was suddenly elated, lifted out of myself by the grandeur of freedom! But I had to quickly make my way to Le Havre to board the ship to Canada.

On ship, I was gripped with a sense of irony. Felice and her husband had wanted with all their hearts to emigrate to the United States to be with Herman. Yet they were on their way to Palestine! I had longed to be in the land, longed to leave Europe with hundreds of my people and be a part of the Return. Yet I was putting my feet on a ship that was bound for the St. Lawrence River and Canadian shores! Only a flimsy telephone promise held out a feeble hope that I would be able to enter the land. Yet I had trusted the Lord for so much: I wasn't going to falter now! Even on the long, lonely journey ahead.

IX

*Entry
into
the Land*

MOMENTS LATER as I was making my way to my cabin, I stared in shock. Pushing her way through the little door inscribed with the number of my "double" cabin was a woman I knew. This woman had traveled with Mary and me from Bratislava all the way to Prague to get a visa for herself for Canada. What dreams we had all shared on that tedious long journey in the compartment of the swaying train!

Now she and I were to travel in the same cabin all the way across the ocean to Canada. It was July 2, 1949. Earlier I had read in the Scriptures and the Lord gave me the verse, "The steps of a good man are ordered by the Lord." Just the presence of a familiar face lifted my heart tremendously and confirmed to me what the Lord had said.

But she was not a Christian and two weeks seemed long to me to be without Christian fellowship. Being in the camps had not conditioned me to be cut off from Christians; it had made me hunger and thirst for fellow-believers. The sweetest thing in the world to me was to share the Scriptures and pray, to sing with those who knew the Savior as I knew Him.

A few days out to sea, I heard an announcement on the loudspeaker that there was to be a Christian prayer meeting. I rushed out of my cabin and onto the deck. There were 100 Mennonites who were emigrating to Canada from the displaced-person camps of Germany. I introduced myself joyfully and asked in some excitement who the speaker would be.

They too were happy and with smiling animation grasped me and began pulling me toward a central place where they were gathered. "You are!" they declared. "You are a missionary! You can speak German!"

That day and every day of the voyage, I was able to minister to them from the Word of God and to share my life and testimony with them.

It became a wonderful journey.

We were all terribly excited when the ship steamed up the mighty St. Lawrence River and into the port of Quebec. I had brought French tracts with me from Paris and had them ready if the Lord gave me an opportunity to witness when I got off the ship.

As the small ship docked, surrounded by a tiny fleet of tugs to guide her into port, I searched the dock for impressions of Canada. To my utter astonishment, there amid the pandemonium of excited people was my Mrs. Gordon, waving as vigorously as her good manners would permit. She had traveled all the way from Montreal to meet my ship.

The summer heat on the dock hit us like a wall. Everything was confusing, and the brusque Canadian English was odd to hear, mixed with the strangely-accented Canadian French. I laughed because everyone English sounded like Margaret and Mrs. Gordon! But Mrs. Gordon made everything simple. She found a hotel for us so I could rest and in a few days, as soon as I was strong enough, she and I boarded the most wonderful train I had ever seen to begin a journey to Toronto. It was the grandest trip I had ever had, and I enjoyed every minute of it to the full. The spacious train was beautiful and spotlessly clean. We had ice water and ice cream and seats like parlor chairs with white towels on the headrest.

As the rugged Canadian wilderness slipped by our windows, I felt I was in a dream. All the sorrows and sufferings and pain of the war years seemed remote for the first time. Only my still aching head was proof that all the agony was not just a nightmare invention.

But all the same, my heart held back. This land was magnificent, but it was not the Promised Land for me. That far country called to me, even across the singing countryside of Canada. I heard the birth pangs of that new nation, torn by war as my Hungary had been—battle-weary, sick, flooded with the homeless of the world. My people. Gladly would I have exchanged the dense coal forests of Ontario for the rocks and burning sand of Palestine.

Mrs. Gordon had no such thoughts. She was eager to take me to all the people who had been praying for my escape from Czechoslovakia. So many had sent letters and prayed. They were eager to meet this "Rose Warmer." Mrs. Gordon had told them about my escape from Communist Czechoslovakia, my survival in the camps, the work I was doing in Europe, the fact that I was a Hebrew Christian. Once I was interviewed by a reporter, and there was a whole page with my picture in a newspaper, an experience I found uncomfortable and unpleasant. But I knew Jewish people would read it and would learn that Jews can believe in Jesus. It was hard to be patient with the journalist; he seemed to feel nothing of what everyone in Europe had gone through. Of course he knew it in his head. But his smooth face and curious eyes could not take in the reality of what I was saying. All the same, I knew the Lord had His reasons for the newspaper story and I tried to forgive the reporter.

The six weeks of my Canadian stay whirled by quickly. Still no document arrived from the Palestinian Consulate in Prague. I hoped to get a visa to go to the United States to see my brother, but it did not come. I realized one morning I had only eight days left.

One day I was invited to a small farm outside Toronto. It was a humble place, lazing in the August heat, the fruit orchards heavy with peaches and apples almost ready for picking.

The Christian brother who owned that farm was greatly concerned about my situation. He had questioned me closely about my plans a few days earlier at the church where I met him and his family. I had smiled at his independent and forthright spirit. "Something ought to be done about this!" he had declared. "I'm going to contact my member of Parliament!"

It seemed to me it was exactly like the times in England.

People there were always talking about writing letters to the government or to the newspapers, wanting things to be put right. In Europe, we had few illusions about such initiative on the part of small people. But in Britain and now in Canada, some fiction persisted that something would happen if one contacted one's "member of Parliament."

On that hot day we sat down to a magnificent farm feast. I marveled at the mounds of food steaming on the table. Flies buzzed on the kitchen screens as if they were too hot to be bothered with the enticing smells from the other side of the room. There was a platter of early corn, bowls of mashed potatoes, sliced beef, gravy, homemade bread, and homemade jam. It was all delicious and astonishing. In Europe, food lines were still very long.

We prayed for God's blessing on the food, and as we raised our heads the telephone rang. The brother left the table and in an instant was back. It was his member of Parliament! The humble farmer was so gratified, his face beamed with pride. "He read your story in the paper, Rose, and wants us to come right over and see him. That's a fine thing, eh?"

All that food was left to cool for the flies. We rushed to the car and made a short journey to the grand home of this government official. He was a very gracious man, almost European in his courtesy, and he asked me many questions. He said he would try to get my visa extended, but he wondered what I valued most in Canada. What did I like most about the country?

I didn't have to think an instant. "Freedom!" I tried to explain to him what it meant for humans to be shut up in a concentration camp; what it was like to be imprisoned within a Communist country. But in Canada, even though I was only a visitor, I was free!

There was a telephone by his elbow on the desk. With an elegant movement he dialed a number. "Ottawa," he said as if that explained everything. While I was sitting there, in a matter of a few minutes he had arranged for a six-week extension of my Canadian visa.

"Perhaps this will allow time for word to come for you from Prague, or the United States," he said as we parted. All of us walked out of his home on air! How wonderfully and how easily the Lord had arranged it all.

Mrs. Gordon took advantage of the extra time by arranging for me to return to Montreal. There were many people there and some churches who had been praying for me. She hadn't known if there would be time for me to meet all these people, but now we must go.

Many times I would have liked to rest. My health was frail Often my whole body ached impossibly and I needed to lie down. But we went to Montreal, and the Lord gave me many opportunities to teach and witness and share all that He had done for me.

It was while we were in Montreal, Canada, that incredibly my visa to Palestine arrived. It was from Bratislava and was actually signed by the local rabbinate. Later I learned that they had even written to the Chief Rabbi in Palestine, telling him that even though I was a missionary I was still a Jew and wanted to emigrate.

The visa's arrival was such a wonderful moment. It seemed too good to be true. We wept. We laughed. We praised God. Over and over I read the letter until Mrs. Gordon said I would go blind or wear the page out.

I suddenly thought of Herman. The Lord knew I was longing to see this brother who had left Europe so long ago. Would the Lord send me forever to Palestine without seeing Herman? I had an ungrateful pang of misgiving. Quickly I asked the Lord to forgive me. I was in His hands, and all that He did was good. Was wonderful!

How wonderful, I was to find out very shortly. Another letter came. It contained my visa to the U.S.A.

Everyone said how profitable it would be for me to be able to visit America! I could meet many more people who had prayed for me. I could visit the Millers. I could speak in many places. There would be no hurry. My visa was for six months. But all I could think of was Herman!

It was a magnificent reunion. After so many years I drank in his every feature, his strong hands and back, his good health! Of all the boys, he was the only one left! How precious he was. I couldn't tell him. Words failed me. I was so grateful to him for living, for being alive and visible after all that had happened to our family.

So the Lord granted me this great joy. For long hours I was also able to tell Herman that Felice and I believed in Jesus as Messiah. Herman had never met a Christian before until he met me, his own sister. It was strange for him and difficult. He was beginning to understand, until one evening at a meeting a speaker pressed my brother, calling him a sinner and saying he had to accept Christ as his Savior. My brother was deeply offended and to my grief, closed his mind completely. He continued to be very kind to me, and my Christian friends were always welcome in his home, but he would not listen to the gospel.

In the months in America, I was reunited with the Millers, and with Karl, who was now a pastor (and was still sending parcels faithfully to all the European believers he could), and met with the many people who had prayed for me all the way throughout the war.

What had been an ordeal in Europe—being refused direct emigration to Palestine—was the Lord's blessing on my future life. I have learned many times that tragedies that seem insurmountable turn out to be the greatest benefits.

In Canada first, and then in America, I was meeting hundreds of people who wanted to pray for me and to know about how I would manage my work in Palestine. Many were thrilled that I was going to the new State of Israel, to be a witness there. Some of the people I met were people who had prayed years for my Christian growth and my safety in wartime Europe. When I was taken to the camps, they prayed all through those horrors that I would survive. And now I met them face to face. It was deeply moving. I often told of the miraculous things that happened to me in the camps, because I felt they were due to the prayers of those very people.

But a strange thing was happening. In letter after letter, Felice warned me against coming to the new State of Israel. At first she expressed doubts. Things were very difficult in Israel. Thousands and thousands of people were pouring into the country day after day. They were living in primitive tents. There were no jobs, there was little food. Even water was very scarce and there was suffering.

Felice had trained as a nurse in the war and with her experience as a therapist helping the doctors of Piešťany, she was about to get a job in Israel as a nurse. But it was a very hard life.

When I wrote in return that the Lord wanted me in Israel, Felice begged me not to come. I had already suffered enough. I didn't know Hebrew. There would be no doctors or hospitals to take care of me. Everyone was sick. It was unbearably hot and humid.

At the same time that Felice bombarded me with pleas not to come, many people urged me to remain in North America. There were Jewish missions that wanted me to stay. People offered to help me get Canadian or American citizenship.

Many times in those busy American days, I had to withdraw and fast and seek the Lord. I knew it was His will for me to return. But I was distressed by the urgency of Felice's sensible letters, and by the logic of the Americans who wanted me to stay.

Felice spared no details in telling of her life in a small room miles from the hospital where she worked. After a long day she would have to walk all the way home, arriving exhausted. In the terrible heat of summer she had a tiny room and a small hot oil stove. She described cooking in that oven of a room, her hungry teenaged boys and husband waiting while the burning sun streamed through the windows.

I began to despair. Finally I went to a pastor and asked him what he thought I ought to do. I shall never forget his counsel: "Never mind listening to what people say! Listen to the Lord and do what He says!" I was so grateful, because that was exactly what I have always wanted to do.

My mind was made up. I was going to Israel!

On August 1, 1950, I boarded an airplane in New York to make the thirty-six-hour flight to Tel Aviv. It was my first experience with flying. My mind was blazing with the realization that I was going to the land of my Lord, the Holy Land, the land of my people! I was in a fever of impatience. It couldn't be true! It couldn't happen at last that I myself would be a part of the prophetic Return!

The longing of our Jewish people for a land of our own had never died in the 1,878 years between the destruction of the Second Temple and the recreation of the State of Israel. For centuries, millions of Jews had prayed that Jerusalem would be restored to them. Jewish pilgrims for hundreds of years had come from Europe to die—to be close to the Holy Temple on resurrection day. When they arrived and their failing eyes saw the devastation of the holy city, it was traditional for them to say the words, "Zion has become a desert, Jerusalem a wilderness," and tear a small rip as long as a finger on a coat or shirt.

During those long barren centuries, perhaps it seemed that Palestine would never be more than a primitive land only good for a Jewish burial ground. But in the beginning of the twentieth century, the impulse had arisen, vague and groping, among Russian Jews for liberation. Many Jews fled Russia—not to Palestine, but to America. But some Jews, fervent with passionate rhetoric, founded a "back to Zion" agricultural movement. It was called the BILU, from the Hebrew initials of the biblical phrase, "House of Jacob, come, let us go!"

Thus, the very first "Aliyah"—the Hebrew word for "ascent," which was used for emigration—began. Russian "lovers of Zion" went ashore at Jaffa by bribing Turkish officials to overlook the ban on Jews entering the land. The Arabs came to call these heroic people *Awlad al Mout* —"Children of Death"—because of the tragic toll on life taken by the white hot climate, malaria, and murdering raids of local inhabitants. But a beginning was made. Jews were coming home to their land!

Our plane droned onward, pulsing through the endless skies that separated us from Israel. On board, people were quiet, lost in their own private agonies and anxieties. An intensity gripped the cabin, lit by sudden flashes of excitement that came and went like the lightning we sometimes saw from the plane's windows.

Everyone's inner eye was turned to one single spot: the landing strip at Tel Aviv where we would first touch down on the soil of our new State.

My thoughts turned to my famous countryman, Theodor Herzl, a Budapest-born lawyer who became struck with the idea of a Jewish homeland somewhere in the world. By the end of the nineteenth century, the idea of Palestine as the homeland had been decided upon. A Jewish National Fund was set up to buy land in Palestine as the property of the entire Jewish people.

I couldn't help smiling at how naive such an idea seemed. Yet from 1904 to the start of World War I, thousands of Jews did go to Palestine, in answer to the Zionist call, and to escape renewed persecutions and massacres in Russia. This was the second

Aliyah. Every Jew knew that among those dedicated pioneers had been a young Polish boy named David Ben-Gurion. He once wrote, "The spirit of my childhood and my dreams had triumphed and was joyous! I was in the land of Israel, in a Jewish village . . . The howling of jackals in the vineyards; the braying of donkeys in the stables . . . the murmur of the distant sea; the darkening shadows of the groves; the enchantment of stars in the deep blue; the faraway skies, drowsily bright—everything intoxicated me."

A rush of emotion welled within me as I thought of young Ben-Gurion coming into the land. He was now the Prime Minister of the State of Israel. No one near me on the plane was concerned at the sudden tears that poured down my cheeks. Soon I myself would hear the braying of donkeys and see the olive groves of Israel! Never mind that Felice described the squalor of the tent camps and flimsy shacks and the cacophony of languages. Never mind that food and water was scarce, and that Jews from Iran and China, Turkey and East Europe by the thousands had somehow to get on together. The skies of Israel would be over my head and her earth under my feet. My spirit exulted in the Lord and how he had brought me so far and through so much to the land. My own land!

It was not without cost. When on May 14, 1948, David Ben-Gurion announced the creation of the State of Israel, every able Jew in the land became a soldier. I had seen pictures of little village boys defending their homes with enormous rifles. People fought with anything at hand. Some fought Arab tanks with stones. The Jewish people had had no army of their own since 135 A.D. when Bar-Kochba led them on the last uprising against Rome. Yet in our war of independence, after all those hundreds of years, Jews marched once again under Jewish generals who called out their orders in Hebrew! Against the armies of five Arab nations they fought—Egypt, Transjordan, Iraq, Syria, and Lebanon. Against armies sworn to annihilate Israel they fought, and they won. Perhaps the world braced itself for the tragic outcome: the poor Jews, once again. But the State of Israel had triumphed. The terror of the crematoria was too vivid a memory, the dreadful camps in Cyprus, the ships turned back from Palestine's shores, for there to be any question of defeat. Six million Jews had perished from the face of the earth. The 700,000 now in Israel would not be lost.

Israel! Our homeland! Never again!

The plane dipped suddenly, and there was a gasp that swept through the plane. Everyone was at the windows, packed on top of each other for the first glimpse of the coastline of Israel. People began weeping and praying in Yiddish and all the languages I had ever heard. Everyone was weeping, embracing.

The blood thundered in my head. "Blessed be the Lord God of Israel, who has brought us safely into the land! Blessed be the Lord God. Holy is his name. Hear, O Israel, the Lord thy God is One!"

It was a hot summer dawn when I stepped from the plane, down the swaying metal stairs to the runway. I was in a sea of confusion and emotion. In spite of the noise of cheering, laughing, weeping all around me, I remembered Mary's clear, sweet voice. "If you ever get out of this country, kiss the ground you come to."

My foot touched the pavement. I was automatically a citizen. Hitler had not prevailed. I was living proof that God remained faithful to His people. Tears of happiness streamed down my face. In a blur of blue I saw above me the Star of David proudly billowing in the morning sky. I was part of the Promise! I had returned.

From a tormented part of my mind came the chant I had heard from those entering the gas chambers at Auschwitz. "*Ani ma'amin be'emuna shlema beviat ha-Mashiah* (I believe in perfect faith in the coming of the Messiah)!" I had returned, but the best of us did not return.

I would not fail their memory, nor the One who had his own Auschwitz on a cross so many centuries before. My hand tightened around the little Bible I was carrying. I had much work to do.

Epilogue

IN THE EARLY DAYS of the State of Israel, Rose discovered that "The Promised Land" was almost a title of irony. For the thousands upon thousands of new immigrants, hardships multiplied. Housing shortages were critical. Scorching summer heat and the biting wet cold of winter had to be endured in primitive crowded facilities. Food was scarce and unvaried. A babel of languages split the air.

Yet the new peoples of Israel endured, strove, and triumphed. Slowly the dusty, broken land was laced with miles of water sprays that yielded tentative, then sturdy crops. Trees took root. The land and its people, reviving to the distant song of an ancient vow, grew strong. Even surrounded by enemies, with vigilance the daily price of survival, Israel prevailed and prospered.

But from the window of a crowded mission bedroom on Mount Carmel, Rose's first view of the land was that of a teeming immigration camp sprawled under the ancient olive trees of the mountain. Immediately she determined that Scripture portions had to be obtained to distribute to the families massed together in the summer heat. Many were from her own Eastern Europe. Letter writing began, appealing to Christians in North America for help.

Rose became settled in the months ahead in a tiny prefab house sent from friends in America (a house, often crowded with guests, that was to be her permanent home). A few people she had met in the United States and Canada sent small gifts of money and food. Money or not, Rose continued to minister in the camps and new settlements, corresponding with Bible societies and missions, asking for portions of Scripture in all the languages of the immigrants.

Supplied by organizations including the Million Testament Campaign, Bible Literature International, the Bible Meditation League, the Pocket Testament League, and national Bible societies, thousands of Scriptures, licensed for import by the government of Israel, were distributed.

The Hebrew Christian Fellowship of Philadelphia learned of her efforts and provided help as early as 1954. In 1958, Rose became a missionary of this organization, although still receiving the encouragement, prayers, and support of individual Christians and organizations—contacts not only in North America, but also in Britain, Sweden, and other countries in which she had traveled.

Her vision reached far beyond Mount Carmel and her city of Haifa. All Israel must be blanketed with God's Word. First driving a tiny scooter loaded with sacks of Scripture, Rose crisscrossed the country, giving out literature to the new schools, *kibbutzim*, factories, and apartment blocks that were springing up all over the land.

Eventually a car was procured, and sometimes helpers came to assist in the work. Her car itself became a mobile chapel, filled with hitchhikers who heard what she had to say and received Scripture.

Illness had to be ignored, as did lack of funds and materials, fatigue, occasional insults and rejection.

"Where were you when my people were in the ovens?" a person might shout as Rose extended a Bible.

Memories would almost strangle the answer: "I was there." No more needed to be said.

At sixty-nine, Rose has lived for the past year in a comfortable nursing home in Haifa. Her health, poor since the camps, no longer permits her the arduous missionary travels throughout her land. She continues a ministry of encouragement, Bible study, and distribution.

It has been a long journey, full of adventures, terrors, hardships, joys. And she is nearly safely home.